Your Résumé : A "Crash Course 2

Résumé Writing from a Christian Perspective for Christian Workers

ISBN # 1442157844
EAN-13 # 9781442157842

So Little Time, So Much to Learn!©

<u>Dear Christian "Crash Course" Client:</u>

<u>Your complete résumé study course "package" includes:</u>
- Introduction
- In-depth skills assessment workshop with compilation of assessment tools
- In-depth résumé writing workshop with "How-to" study course on résumé writing condensed from the *Your Résumé : A "Crash Course"*© group workshop
- Compilation of résumé writing tools
- Sample résumés for Christian workers
- Sample resignation letter and cover letters, with writing instructions
- Résumé survey chart

Also available in the *YRACC*© Tools Online Add-on Digital Component:
- Career goal analysis tools
- Other job-search tools

Go to http://www.wordcopro.com for details and ordering information for the Online Add-on Digital Component

YRACC 2©

Résumé Writing from a Christian Perspective

STUDY COURSE CONTENTS

INTRODUCTION TO *Your Résumé : A "Crash Course" 2*© *Résumé Writing from a Christian Perspective*

<u>Why write another résumé book</u> when there are so many on the market already? The "simple answer" — when I first saw that writing résumés was going to be a major part of the desktop publishing business I opened in 1987, I set out to learn everything I could about résumé writing. As I read book after book, it became abundantly clear that no single one of them contained everything I needed to know.

> Virtually any job search in your lifetime will be a fairly high-stress period, and the additional stress of having to come up with a competitive résumé is undesirable at best – *even if you're completely confident that God has His hand on every aspect and area of the project*.

When I was asked in the early 1990s to teach résumé writing in a college English class, I had to sit down and figure out how to teach college students all that I had learned. Because of time constraints, I had to "weed out all the fluff" and teach only the very most important aspects of résumé writing. After several years of refinement and editing, the end result was my three-hour group workshop.

This book is an outtake of that workshop, targeted toward helping a Christian individual, seeking ministry or missions opportunities, to learn the absolute most important things I have learned in 22+ years of writing résumés.

<u>Not just another résumé book</u>. Many résumé books completely leave out the most important step in résumé writing — recognizing and describing your God-given gifts, talents, skills and abilities. We're all too busy for "one more thing" to do, so this study course is purposely organized to quickly teach you to "do it yourself".

The *Your Résumé : A "Crash Course"*© *2* study course is intended to rapidly provide you with all of the tools necessary to prepare for, complete and print a "professional" résumé (You have to provide the word processor/printer or typewriter and some quality paper). You will find simple, but in-depth, tools specifically designed to assess your God-given skills, knowledge and abilities; information-gathering tools, and complete résumé writing instructions; plus a form to track where you've sent your résumés (and the responses you've received).

And if you've purchased the "Online Tools Add-on Component", you will also be studying your way through additional career-related tools (some of them very fun and interesting) to teach you about interviewing, career values and job searches.

Help !!! More often than you might think, the people who take advantage of my professional résumé service or attend my résumé writing workshops have just been to the library to check out every book available on résumé writing, have purchased (and READ) books on résumé writing at the book store, have purchased (and used) résumé writing software, have researched on the Internet (or all of the above) and are *still* confused and skeptical about documenting their "worklives". By the time they get to me, clients often are, in effect, at their wits' end and desperate for help! Virtually any job search in your lifetime will be a fairly high-stress period, and the additional stress of having to come up with a competitive résumé is undesirable at best. My aim is to offer you God-given tools that may help to cut that stress to a manageable level. We all know that it is not God's desire for us to be "stressed" about anything.

Ministry and missions résumés add yet another element to the "mix" because they aren't written from the same perspective as the résumé of a secular job-seeker. With a missions or ministry résumé, you are explaining God's call on your life and how it fits into the needs and wants of the ministry, church or missions organization to which you will be sending the résumé and statement of beliefs. You are demonstrating who you are in Christ and how you have served Him in the past. You will also be sharing how you hope to serve Him in the future – where you believe He is currently leading you.

In addition to other trouble areas, it is very difficult for many people to be *objective* about their own skills and abilities and get them down on paper. Perhaps it shouldn't be; but it is, nonetheless. It is nothing short of amazing how many people, even today with the increased resources at hand and opportunities for learning, don't feel comfortable writing a résumé for themselves. And knowing "how" and being able to actually DO it are not necessarily one and the same, either.

By design, the skills assessment tools and organizational forms in this study course will help give you that extra "edge" to be able to successfully do your own résumé where others can not. It would likely surprise you the number of my résumé clients who are executives and supervisors who read tens and sometimes hundreds of résumés every month and know EXACTLY what a

> Think how rewarding it will be to be able to say, "God enabled me to do it myself."

résumé should look like and what THEY [as either an employer, a human resources director, or a department head/supervisor] like to see on a résumé; and they still hire me to write their résumé for them.

Let's face it — it's not as simple as it may sound to document *an entire job, either secular or missions/ministry-related, in one or two brief paragraphs*, and *an entire history* in one or two brief pages (you will find argument here and there against it, but résumés may occasionally be three pages if the information they contain is all pertinent — I got that from a VERY reliable source!). I'll teach you how to record your service as briefly as possible.

I kid you not, in the last 30+ years that I've been in the business world, as well as during the 22+ that I've been writing résumés professionally, I've seen some REALLY lousy résumés; and entirely too many of them came from high-priced "résumé services". The adage "you get what you pay for" does NOT always apply! Many résumés I've reviewed (and REDONE) that were generated by supposedly "professional" résumé services weren't worth the paper they were written on, much less the *up to $300.00* people paid for them. It's a genuine shame when someone has to put up with *typographical errors and poorly represented information* in a résumé that cost that much money (or ANY money for that matter, really)! With a little guidance (and a lot of prayer), that won't happen to you.

Teaching an "Old Dog New Tricks". No, I'm not saying anybody reading this book is an "old dog". However, résumé writing is a skill virtually anyone of any age beyond middle school can learn with a healthy dose of good information, specific examples, and a little practice. You will have to use (and maybe develop) all of your *organizational writing skills* (never mind that you didn't know you had any), make judgments on format, and check carefully for errors (don't be shy about asking friends and/or relatives for help in proofing your completed work – you SHOULD ask others to review it). And never mind that you're nervous about being up to this task — that's normal. God will get you through it. If it's really bothering you, ask your prayer group to lift every aspect of your search up in prayer, including the résumé-writing phase. **[Philippians 4:13 *I can do all things through Him who strengthens me."*]**

Here's an important point to consider. It truly is *to your advantage to write your résumé yourself* rather than hiring it done. Think how rewarding it will be to be able to say, "God enabled me to do it myself," in response to questioning from an impressed interviewer! In recent years, I have focused primarily on writing résumés for Christians because I believe I have been called to assist God's people in getting to the next "appointment" He has in His plan for them.

It is clear there is a niche for this book. There is a huge difference between answering God's call on your life and applying for a job. That has to be reflected in the assessment, formatting, and wording a Christian uses.

It's time for you to get started with your pre-résumé assessments. Please be sure to undertake this activity seriously and honestly.

Gretchen Slinker Jones

> "I hereby swear that the information contained in the attached résumé is true and correct to the best of my knowledge."
> Matthew Missionary

SECTION ONE

⧫

THE SKILLS ASSESSMENT WORKSHOP

SKILLS ASSESSMENT | PART ONE

RECOGNITION AND ANALYSIS OF SKILLS. Whether we like to think of it that way or not, seeking the fulfillment of God's next call on your life is advertising and marketing a "product" — YOU. We're not used to thinking of ourselves as products, and it's harder for some than others to embrace the idea. Any top salesman will tell you that step one is to <u>know your product.</u>

Assess
Analyze
Recognize
Quantify
Qualify

Churches or organizations making a critical (and perhaps expensive and/or time consuming) decision whether or not to call or hire you don't just want to receive a list of your former employers and job titles. They want to know how you are answering God's call on your life and whether what you believe will be in line with their doctrinal statement and core beliefs. In today's tighter economy, it is often necessary for pastors, missionaries, music directors, worship leaders and others to take on multiple roles and/or responsibilities in their Christian service. Knowing how many ways you might be used of the Lord is essential – for both you <u>and</u> the prospective church or organization.

Although we don't usually give it much thought, the average adult has *several hundred* skills that are transferable to a fairly wide variety of applications, as well as very specific skills that have predetermined applications. The majority of people have a hard time both identifying and quantifying their skills, however; primarily because, although all of us could cite examples to the contrary, by nature, most of us are genuinely humble people. Self-assessment is much more a part of primary, secondary, and post-secondary education today than it was when many of us were growing up, so the "younger generation" tends to be more capable of recognizing their skills and abilities. It's almost ridiculously simple. A skill is anything you can do.

Please note that none of the skills assessment activities in this book originate with me. You're not "buying" them — you're buying my expertise on résumé writing. These activities are a compilation and adaptation of the most useful materials I have found among those widely available in online searches over the past 15 years. I have included them to save you hours and hours of perusing the 30,000,000 entries that come up when you type "skills assessment" in an Internet search box. If you have lots of "spare time", feel free to search online for additional skills assessment tools. There are literally thousands of websites, many of them connected with colleges and universities, containing career- or job-related skills assessment tools. I don't think it is possible to know too much about recognizing, assessing, and conveying information regarding your skills, abilities, and knowledge base to a prospective church, organization, or employer, so if you have time, please consider doing some further research and study in that area.

The job market of the future is guaranteed to be more and more competitive — and not just in "white-collar" jobs, but in the trades and service industries as well. And if you're changing career fields – or moving into full-time ministry from volunteer or part-time service, it is even more critical that you fully understand the skills and abilities you possess so you can determine whether they will qualify you for new areas of responsibility. Two main types of skills are: job skills and self-management skills.

Job Skills are those specific to a job or occupation. An accountant, for example, might be skilled in some or all of these areas:

1. accounts receivable, accounts payable, and/or payroll
2. tax reporting
3. proficiency with one or more computer accounting software applications
4. ability to compile and prepare detailed analysis reports
5. tax preparation, either manual or with software applications

A music director might make use of some of these skills:

1. read and understand music
2. play one or more instruments
3. work effectively with persons of all ages and backgrounds
4. schedule rehearsals and events
5. recruit musicians and/or singers
6. develop programs

A secretary, administrative assistant or receptionist, might list:

1. word processing (hardly anyone uses a typewriter these days)
2. filing
3. answering telephones (including multi-phone systems)
4. distributing correspondence (yes, the mail still comes to the office)
5. greeting clients (a timeless skill)

And you don't acquire or learn job/occupational skills simply from working. You are likely to develop transferable job skills (those skills that can be useful in many different occupations) through involvement or participation in education, hobbies, community activities, volunteer work — even from what may seem, on first thought, to be "common", everyday life experiences.

I would strongly encourage you to write out an example of each as it pertains to your work "life" and/or ministry or missions focus. Use a piece of paper if you don't want to write in your book.

Self-Management Skills are everyday skills you use to interact with other people (both in and out of your company/organization) and to accomplish tasks or perform functions. **[Galatians 5:22 *"But the fruit of the Spirit is love, joy, peace, patience, kindness, goodness, faithfulness, gentleness, self-control …"*]** They involve using self-control in dealing with the people around you, time spent at work (and other activities) and in your "environment" — skills like:

1. Sincerity

2. Reliability

3. Tactfulness

4. Patience

5. Flexibility

6. Timeliness

Especially in ministry and missions "occupations", the fruits of the Spirit produce desirable qualities in those who are called to the Lord's service in many capacities. There are practical qualities desirable in all employees in all fields, as well.

Give an example if you can you honestly say that you are:

1. Punctual?

2. Conscientious?

3. Imaginative?

4. Loyal?

5. Sincere?

6. Efficient?

7. Dependable?

8. Industrious?

9. A team player?

10. A good listener?

Fruit of the Spirit
"... love, joy, peace, patience, kindness, goodness, faithfulness, gentleness, self-control ..."

Basic skills will be incorporated into any type of work or service to the Lord you will ever do over your lifetime. Although they do vary from career field to career field, occupation to occupation and job to job, they more often than not will include at least most of those listed below. As a result of numerous studies on the subject, experts, without question, agree that persons of all ages and backgrounds working in every job in today's workplace should have <u>at least an average command of all of these skills</u>. Christian workers are not excluded from this!

Write in ONE example of how you have used each of these skills in previous or current positions, either paid or volunteer (or at school if you are still a student).

➤ <u>Reading for information</u> (correspondence, bulletins, instruction manuals, policies and procedures; graphs, charts and displays; critiquing someone else's work)

➤ <u>Applied mathematics</u> (Understanding and solving math problems and being able to use the results)

➤ <u>Locating Information</u> (finding information in company files, internet or library research, using catalogues to answer client questions or determine product availability or pricing information)

➤ <u>Applied Technology</u> (Using various computer hardware/software applications)

➤ <u>Communicating</u> (Understanding, speaking, reading and writing in the language in which the business is conducted)

> **Thinking** (Thinking critically and acting logically to evaluate situations, solve problems and make decisions)

> **Listening** to understand and learn (attending meetings, receiving instructions in person or over the phone, taking customer orders)

> **Teamwork** (Planning and making decisions with others and supporting the outcomes, respecting the thoughts and opinions of others in the group, exercising "give and take" to achieve group results, leading when appropriate)

> **Learning** (Continue to learn for life)

> **Adaptability** (Having a positive attitude toward change, respecting people's diversity, identifying and suggesting new ideas to get the job done)

Which two of these have you used most in the past?

Which two would you most like to do better?

SKILLS IDENTIFICATION AND ANALYSIS
'CEMENT YOUR KNOWLEDGE" WORKSHEET

I would guess that there's a lot more to this "skills thing" than you thought. ***Please answer the following questions based on what you have just read in this activity***; then think back through your life, both in and out of the workplace, and LIST at least 20 skills you have and indicate what you believe is your skill level on each (**Experienced, Capable or Beginner**). You may list more than 20 if you want to.

How many skills does the average person have?

What are the two MAIN types of skills?

    1. _____

    2. _____

There are ten types of **basic skills** outlined. Please name FIVE of them:

    1. _____

    2. _____

    3. _____

    4. _____

    5. _____

Which TWO of those five listed above do you believe to be your strongest of the five:

    1. _____

    2. _____

Brainstorming Time.

On the next page, make a listing of at least twenty of your own skills. Next to the skill name, write E for Experienced, C for Capable, or B for Beginner to describe the level of this skill you currently possess. If you are currently in training in this skill area (whether on the job or in a college or tech school), write T next to the skill.

Feel free to write down more than 20 skills. Acknowledging your gifts is allowed!

YOUR CURRENT SKILLS: (Experienced, Capable, Beginner, or in Training)

_____   _____
_____   _____
_____   _____
_____   _____
_____   _____
_____   _____
_____   _____
_____   _____
_____   _____
_____   _____
_____   _____
_____   _____
_____   _____

Are there additional skills you would ultimately like to receive training for in the next five years?   YES   NO

If YES, please list them below:

_____   _____
_____   _____
_____   _____

Where and how might you receive this training?

If it will cost money, approximately how much?

SKILLS ASSESSMENT | PART TWO

As you have already learned, it is difficult for most people to objectively assess their own skills, abilities and knowledge, let alone to **express those skills to others**. The purpose of this assignment is not only to further help you learn to *objectively assess your own skills and abilities*, but to teach you to honestly and accurately *convey your level of expertise in those skills and abilities to someone else* in a meaningful and effective manner. It is a prerequisite to the Résumé Information WorkSheet Activity you will be doing further on in this study course.

- Read
- Understand
- Answer
- Complete
- Write

Please understand this: No matter what you think you already know about yourself and your abilities, you can't do your best résumé if you haven't thoroughly assessed your skills, knowledge and abilities. *Make sure you check off ALL THREE parts below as you complete the assignment so you don't miss part of it!*

Answer the questions and provide details honestly based on your skills and abilities as they are TODAY. This is NOT a hypothetical activity.

❑ Read the information provided and answer the questions.

❑ Complete the "Skills and Abilities" worksheets that apply to your particular situation. You may make ONE copy of the worksheets in this study course if you prefer not to write in the book.

❑ Complete the "Skills Statement" activity, including the actual writing of your individual skills statement. Space is provided in this book if you wish to handwrite your statement (some companies request a sample of a prospective employee's handwriting, so this could be good practice). You are welcome to do it on your computer rather than handwrite it. Almost all of the time, Christian workers are asked to provide some form of theological statement. This exercise can be expanded to fulfill that purpose, as well.

NOTE: Please do not be tempted to skip around through these activities. They are set up purposely to progressively achieve the desired result.

What Can You Do?
It's Time To Begin Seriously Assessing Your Current Skills and Abilities

> An important second step in this process is recognizing and quantifying your accomplishments and strengths.

It is virtually impossible for you to write a thorough résumé or convince a pastoral search committee or an interviewer to call or hire you until you not only fully review <u>what you KNOW and CAN DO</u>, but can effectively EXPRESS your skills and knowledge both on paper and orally <u>to someone else</u>. Working your way through this self-assessment exercise will help you identify and communicate your current skills on your résumé and cover letter, as well as in an interview.

Each time I sit down with a résumé client to "pick his or her brain", by the end of the session, the client is amazed at the depth and breadth of what he or she knows and can do! Frankly, they just haven't ever been made fully aware of the scope of what they know and can do. One would assume this is primarily because the majority of our skills and abilities are acquired over long periods of time and through many varied activities.

This activity is not about job entries that will appear on a résumé — it is about working your way through ALL past experiences to summarize what you know and can offer your next employer. You will, however, be able to include some of the information you map out here directly on your résumé.

In the following exercises, keep in mind all previous jobs <u>(both paid and volunteer</u>) you have had, plus any community and leisure-time activities you have participated in. (And PLEASE don't limit yourself to the sampling of possibilities included here!)

For working adults, possibilities include:

- ❖ Paid positions in any career area, of course
- ❖ Elected or appointed as an officer of a church
- ❖ Volunteering at church camps, mission trips, VBS, or retreat events
- ❖ Teaching church school classes
- ❖ Caring for elderly or invalid parents, children or other family members
- ❖ Elected or appointed as an officer of a civic club or organization (Lions, Elks, Eagles, Rotary, Chamber of Commerce, etc.)

- ❖ TEACHING or FACILITATING work-related seminars, conferences or workshops
- ❖ Attending work-related seminars, conferences or workshops (write them down even if they took place many years ago)
- ❖ Coaching sports teams
- ❖ Volunteering as a non-officer in civic organizations and/or activities
- ❖ Special or extraordinary projects accomplished at a job
- ❖ Hobbies or avocations
- ❖ Teaching community education classes, either for pay or as a volunteer

For high school and/or college students with little work experience, possibilities include:

- ❖ teaching Sunday School
- ❖ helping out at a summer camp (church, VBS, 4-H, scouts, etc.)
- ❖ participating in either paid or non-paid school-to-work courses or internships in high school or college
- ❖ tutoring, either paid or as a volunteer
- ❖ elected or appointed as class or club officer
- ❖ serving as statistician, coach or manager, or player on a sports team
- ❖ babysitting or caring for a grandparent
- ❖ working on the annual staff
- ❖ providing tech or lighting support or backstage help for a drama group
- ❖ acting in a play or other production
- ❖ summer or part-time jobs
- ❖ helping with a family-operated business
- ❖ teaching ski school, dance or music lessons
- ❖ serving as DJ at school dances
- ❖ spending time as community volunteer
- ❖ volunteering in hospital or nursing home
- ❖ participating in fund-raising activities such as car washes, or sales of baked goods, candy, magazines, etc.
- ❖ Students, if you have done (or now do) regular chores at home, you may list those as a "job" and write down the information the same as any "job". Your "supervisor" would be the parent who let you know whether or not you were doing the work satisfactorily.

An important second step in this process is recognizing and quantifying your accomplishments and strengths. To state it simply, _accomplishments are those activities that, upon recollection, give you a sense of fulfillment or success_. They can be large or small in scope; routine or extraordinary; frequent or something you have done only once; work related or personal.

[University of British Columbia. www.landfood.ubc.ca/careers/documents/get_prep_self_assess.pdf]

In the next few pages, you will cement what you have learned and then assess your skills and abilities by filling out as many columns as are appropriate for your own circumstances on the charts toward the end of this assignment.

The "Skills and Abilities" portion of the assignment includes three separate categories of experience in which you likely have gained skills and abilities. They are (1) Actual Paid Positions, (2) Volunteer Positions and (3) Attending (or Facilitating) Workshops, Seminars or Conferences. This exercise is an excellent tool to gather your thoughts, see what you have done and what you know mapped out in "black and white" right in front of your eyes, and appraise their importance (or perhaps unimportance) to your future worklife or ministerial call.

When you get to that part of the activity, please do yourself a favor and take the time to answer all questions in each column you begin. Do not leave any blanks in the column. Be as thorough as possible. This should be a serious brainstorming activity targeted to producing the best possible résumé. Use an additional sheet of paper if you have more than four in any category.

> This activity isn't about job entries that will appear on a résumé ...

SKILLS ASSESSMENT "CEMENT YOUR KNOWLEDGE" WORKSHEET –
(1) FOR OLDER, EXPERIENCED WORKING ADULTS

From the list of possible jobs or activities on the previous pages where you might have gained the skills that you now have, name 10 possible places you may have learned skills yourself:

1.
2.
3.
4.
5.
6.
7.
8.
9.
10.

List and briefly describe any seminars or workshops you have attended in the last 5 years (or previous to that if they pertain to the work you are seeking).

Have you trained co-workers or new employees? Describe:

Are one-time or periodic certifications required in your line of work? List:

List and briefly describe any specific on-the-job training you have received that will be useful in the future.

List and briefly describe any community volunteer services such as assisting with a VBS venture (either in your own church or someone else's), summer camps, hospital or nursing home volunteer, helping an elderly or disabled parent/grandparent, or other volunteer work such cemetery clean-up crew, state or local fair set-up, work on a community parade float, assisting in a homeless shelter, etc.

SKILLS ASSESSMENT "CEMENT YOUR KNOWLEDGE" WORKSHEET
(2) FOR YOUNG WORKING ADULTS OR STUDENTS W/LITTLE EXPERIENCE.

From the list of possible jobs or activities on the previous pages where you might have gained the skills that you now have, name 10 possible places you may have learned skills yourself:

A.
B.
C.
D.
E.
F.
G.
H.
I.
J.

List and briefly describe any full-time work, part-time or summer jobs such as lawn mowing, hay crew, child care, fast food restaurants, high school or college work study or internships, etc.

List and briefly describe any participation in individual or team sports activities.

List and briefly describe any participation in other extra-curricular activities such as academic clubs, service clubs, etc.

List and briefly describe any experience acting in a music or drama production or working on the backstage/support crew of a music or drama production.

List and briefly describe any participation in car washes, bake sales, candy sales, magazine sales or other fund-raising activities.

List and briefly describe any community volunteer services such as assisting with a VBS venture (either in your own church or someone else's), summer camps, hospital or nursing home volunteer, helping an elderly or disabled parent/grandparent, or other volunteer work such cemetery clean-up crew, state or local fair set-up, work on a community parade float, assisting in a homeless shelter, etc.

Workplace Skills

For this activity, please take the time to read and study each point in the list below carefully so you can make an **_accurate_** assessment of how this skill relates to you and the "work" you do (or that you plan to do in the future). It is best to complete the activity according to your current use of skills today, not at some fictional time in the future. Students: If you don't have enough work experience to complete this exercise from an employee's standpoint, you should apply them to your school experiences.

> Can you imagine explaining today's "information superhighway" to someone born in 1895?

Although it changes somewhat from generation to generation (and with ever-increasing age for drawing full Social Security benefits), most individuals will spend at least one-third of their lives working — and no one can dispute that today's workplace is an incredibly diverse and constantly-changing environment. People answering God's call on their lives in ministry or missions often never "retire". They continue serving the Lord in some capacity until He calls them home.

Even if their goals and plans are already thoroughly analyzed and galvanized, people in today's job market (and the job market of the future) will have to continue to demonstrate an understanding of both academics and workplace skills to succeed over the long term. The work world is changing before our eyes; and whether we readily accept it or not, we must change with it or be left standing in the dust of those who did!

Although some attempt to predict what the job market of the future is going to look like, none of us can see tomorrow before it gets here. Can you imagine explaining today's "information superhighway" to someone born in 1895? It hasn't been that many years since there was no such thing as a network administrator or a blog. Even churches today sometimes have network administrators and blogs.

Don't miss the next point, it's very important! Skills are not only learned, but they must be APPLIED to be meaningful. As the result of a cooperative effort between business and industry, community members and school personnel, the following eight areas were developed outlining skills that have been identified as being desirable in a person working in virtually ANY job in today's work world. Information on these cooperative efforts is widely available online. Feel free to do further research on this topic.

INSTRUCTIONS: Read through and mentally prioritize the listed items in each category in terms of what items are used most in the day-to-day work YOU do in your current position (or in a previous job or internship if you are not currently employed or in school if you are not yet employed).

Depending on where and how you have been employed or served in ministry or missions, they may not all apply equally to your situation; but you should attempt to include as many as possible to gain a full understanding of how they apply to you. Evaluate and choose **your** TOP TWO criteria in each category, and **write** the numbers 1 and 2 in the boxes next to those two listed items which you use most yourself. If you don't use any, indicate areas you would like to improve in.

Feel free to make ONE scan or copy of this activity if you prefer not to write in your book. This activity will also refresh or coach you on some vocabulary and terminology you will likely be able to use in writing your résumé.

Communication
Employees use principles of effective oral, written and listening communication skills to make decisions and solve workplace problems.

☐ Communicate a *clear message* and *respond* appropriately to listener feedback

☐ Maintain records and information *completely* and *accurately*

☐ Understand and summarize information from reading material; and be able to express the main points to someone else clearly (either in writing or verbally), using as few words as possible

☐ Judge the accuracy, appropriateness, style and believability of reports, proposals and/or theories; and *convey information* in various specialized fields such as scientific, technical and business in written form appropriate to the audience and *effectively edited* to reflect a solid knowledge of grammar, mechanics and vocabulary

☐ Plan and produce an effective visual technical report or display

☐ Express and defend their points of view by formulating sound, rational arguments and applying the art of persuasion and debate

Computation and Analysis

Employees apply computation skills and data analysis techniques to make decisions and solve workplace problems.

❑ Select and use appropriate computation techniques, such as averaging, estimation, statistical techniques, and appropriate electronic calculations

❑ Use raw data, charts, tables and graphs that summarize data from real-world situations to compute projections

❑ Use appropriate technology to display and analyze workplace data

Critical and Creative Thinking

Employees apply critical and creative thinking skills to make decisions and solve workplace problems.

❑ Come up with alternatives, consider risks, make evaluations and choose solutions

❑ Keep track of progress, evaluate success, and make necessary adjustments to meet established objectives

❑ Look back on and study (interpret) results (or outcome) of an action taken to determine what has been gained, lost or achieved

❑ Recognize a need for data, obtain the data, and develop ways to determine its accuracy

❑ Identify and effectively allocate available resources (e.g. time, money, materials, facilities and human resources)

❑ Monitor, track and evaluate results, coming up with new solutions or persuasively justifying current solutions

❑ Demonstrate the ability to adapt new information to changing situations and requirements

❑ Combine ideas or information in new ways, make connections between seemingly unrelated ideas, and reshape goals in ways that reveal new possibilities to solve problems

❑ Develop an inventory record keeping system to maintain data and information in a systematic fashion

❑ Apply a continuous improvement process to an existing business, process or project

Work Individually and as a Team Member

Employees work individually and collaboratively within team settings to accomplish objectives. They key term here is ACCOMPLISH OBJECTIVES.

- ❑ Negotiate solutions to conflicts, *separating the "people" from the "problem"*; focusing on *interests, not positions*, coming up with options for mutual gain; and insisting on the use of *objective criteria*
- ❑ Work and communicate with a variety of clients, customers and community contacts to satisfy their expectations
- ❑ Pursue difficult and challenging leadership roles

"Marketable" Skills

Employees demonstrate a set of marketable skills that enhance career options.

- ❑ Write, evaluate and revise a career plan consistent with occupational interests, aptitudes and abilities
- ❑ Demonstrate job acquisition skills by completing résumé and job applications and by demonstrating interviewing techniques
- ❑ Consistently exhibit work ethics and behaviors essential for success in all areas of life
- ❑ Demonstrate marketable occupational skills for an entry-level job based on career interests
- ❑ Increase academic and occupational skills when necessary to become more "marketable"
- ❑ Evaluate career plans on a continuing basis to determine if further education, skills or knowledge are necessary for continued success

Understanding Systems

Employees illustrate how social, organizational and technological systems function.

- ❑ Write formal communications that have a definite audience and clear purpose; contain no gaps, omissions or assumptions which get in the way of comprehension; and follow the proper form -- whether it be a personal or business letter, message, memo, manual directions/instructions or applications
- ❑ Exhibit interviewing skills (e.g. responding effectively to questions, using language that conveys maturity, sensitivity and respect; dressing appropriately; and using appropriate body language

- ☐ Respond to verbal and nonverbal messages in ways that show understanding on your part
- ☐ Communicate a clear message and appropriately respond to listener feedback
- ☐ Participate in conversation, discussion and/or group presentations using verbal and nonverbal communication with style and tone that are appropriate for audience and occasion
- ☐ Maintain records and information completely and accurately
- ☐ Create documents (e.g. letters, memos, manuals, graphs, flowcharts, directions, reports and proposals) that are clear; appropriate to the audience, subject matter and purpose; and exhibit the writer's use of correct grammar, spelling and punctuation
- ☐ Respond to informal and formal speeches using illustrations, statistics, comparisons and analogies to critique the effectiveness of those presentations
- ☐ Locate the meaning of unknown or technical vocabulary words/terms by using reason and current knowledge to intelligently research available resources
- ☐ Research and gain understanding of information; then develop a written document to convey only the information that is appropriate to the audience
- ☐ Deliver a polished or impromptu speech that is organized and well suited to the audience, using effective body language and voice inflection to clarify and defend positions
- ☐ Conduct a thoughtful interview, taking appropriate notes and summarizing the information learned
- ☐ Plan and produce an effective visual technical report or display
- ☐ Identify a problem, conduct research, and summarize the findings and solutions, using sources such as technical journals and government publications to support the original thesis
- ☐ Express and defend points of view by formulating sound, rational arguments and applying the art of persuasion and debate

Continued

Technology

Employees demonstrate technological literacy for productivity in the workplace.

❑ Select and use appropriate technology to organize, send and receive information

❑ Study and understand the impact of technological changes on tasks, people and society

❑ Demonstrate computer operations skills such as computer-aided drafting and computer-integrated manufacturing with other technologies in a variety of applications within a workplace setting

❑ Adapt available technology use to expand academic and personal growth

❑ Identify or solve problems with computers and other technologies

Resource Management

Employees apply principles of resource management and develop skills that promote personal and professional well-being.

❑ Set and prioritize goals, *estimate the time required* to complete each assigned task, and prepare and *follow* the timeline/schedule

❑ Prepare a short-and long-term personal budget; make expenditure, income and savings forecasts; and maintain proper records

❑ Evaluate the impact of health choices (e.g. smoking, substance abuse, exercise) on personal and professional well-being

❑ Identify strategies for balancing self, family, work, leisure and citizenship; brainstorm ways to reduce the impact of stress; and understand how both relate to personal and career satisfaction

❑ Maintain a personal management system by setting goals, managing resources, and balancing life choices to accomplish career and life satisfaction

❑ Design a computer-generated workplace document with narrative and graphics, using desktop publishing software.

If you want to really get in-depth with this activity, you could take the most important points from each category and write out examples of how you have applied these principles in one or more previous ministry or work settings. You will have to decide how far you want to go with it.

Especially if you are not in ministry or missions, but ARE a Christian whose desire is to work in any job "as unto the Lord", you will want to give yourself the best possible chance to "win" an interview and ultimately get hired for the position you believe God has for you.

MOST-DESIRABLE WORKPLACE SKILLS

- Communication -
- Computation and Analysis -
- Critical and Creative Thinking -
- Work Individually and as a Team Member -
- "Marketable" Skills -
- Understanding Systems -
- Technology -
- Resource Management -

"With good will render service as to the Lord, and not to men ..."
Ephesians 6:7

Workplace Skills "CEMENT YOUR KNOWLEDGE" Questions

1. We spend approximately what fraction of our lifetime in the workforce?

   _____

2. Skills must not only be learned, but they must be

   _____ .

3. Name the EIGHT skill areas identified by business and industry, schools and communities as being desirable in any working person.

   1.

   2.

   3.

   4.

   5.

   6.

   7.

   8.

4. List the two items you identified as most important in the "Marketable Skills" category:

   1.

   2.

5. List the two items in the whole assessment where you believe you need the most improvement:

   1.

   2.

SKILLS AND ABILITIES. Information Gathering, Step 1 VOLUNTEER

As you begin to identify your skills, list ALL volunteer "jobs" here _even if they may not end up on your résumé_. You may want to broadly summarize some skills/abilities on your résumé and this will help you do that. Fill in all boxes for each entry. Try not to leave any blank spaces. If you need more space, continue on another sheet of paper. You may wish to assess another three or four volunteer positions to see what you know. **Do this BEFORE you do the next part of the activity!!** _You may make a copy of this page if needed._

Information	"Job" 1	"Job" 2	"Job 3"	"Job 4"
Job, project, or activity				
Position or title?				
Your start and end dates				
What did your duties include?				
What was a typical day like?				
What were the consequences of doing your job well?				
What were the consequences of doing your job poorly?				
What did you like most about your work?				
What did you like least about your work?				
What would your supervisor have to say about your work asked about you?				

SKILLS AND ABILITIES. Information Gathering, Step 1 PAID WORK

As you continue to identify your skills, list ALL paid work jobs here *even if they may not end up on your résumé*. Fill in all boxes for each entry. Try not to leave any blank spaces. If you need more space, continue on another sheet of paper. You may need to broadly summarize some skills/abilities on your résumé. **Do this BEFORE you do the next part of the activity!!** *You may make a copy of this page if needed.*

Information	"Job" 1	"Job" 2	"Job 3"	"Job 4"
Job, project, or activity				
Position or title?				
Your start and end dates				
What did your duties include?				
What was a typical day like?				
What were the consequences of doing your job well?				
What were the consequences of doing your job poorly?				
What did you like most about your work?				
What did you like least about your work?				
What would your supervisor have to say about your work if asked about you?				

SKILLS AND ABILITIES. Information Gathering, Step 1
WORKSHOPS/SEMINARS/CONFERENCES, *EITHER AS AN ATTENDEE OR AS A FACILITATOR*

As you finish identifying your skills, list ALL workshops, seminars and conferences here *even if they may not end up on your résumé*. Fill in all boxes for each entry. Try not to leave any blank spaces. If you need more space, continue on another sheet of paper.

Information	Item 1	Item 2	Item 3	Item 4
Workshop, seminar or conference				
What was your capacity?				
When was this?				
What did the studies or activity include?				
What was the primary focus of the event or activity?				
What were the most concrete benefits you gained?				
What would you change about the activity?				
What did you like most about the activity?				
What did you like least about the activity?				
If you were a presenter or facilitator, what kind of evaluation(s) did you receive from participants?				

Skills Statement

Ok, it's cliché, but "It's all about you" – within the parameters of "It's all about God".

> The thoughts you develop in this statement will help you be ready to answer interview questions.
> I Peter 3:15 *"...always being ready to make a defense to everyone who asks you to give an account for the hope that is in you, yet with gentleness and reverence."*

As practicing Christians, we understand that it's never "all about us". This does not, however, exempt us from needing to correctly represent our skills and abilities in the search for God's next call on our lives. **["With good will render service as to the Lord, and not to men ..." – Ephesians 6:7]**

Having an awareness of what you know and can do is just skimming the surface of the skills assessment process. The information we've gathered thus far, in and of itself, is of little use if you can't COMMUNICATE it to someone else who needs to know it (in this case, a prospective church or missions organization, through your résumé, theological or doctrinal statement, and cover letter, as well as during your resulting interview appointment)!

After completing the previous assessment pages, our next step is to prepare a **skills statement** about yourself.

The skills statement is a summary of the skills, abilities, knowledge, and accomplishments you have just reviewed and assessed that briefly, but thoroughly, highlights what you can offer to a company or organization. Your statement will not only increase your own awareness of "you", but it will be of tremendous value as you write a résumé, compose related correspondence, and work your way through the interview process. The thoughts you develop in this statement <u>will help you be ready to answer interview questions</u> such as: "Tell me about yourself". "Why should I hire you"? "What can you offer the organization or company"? *Your thoughtfully crafted statement will help you answer such questions with confidence.* **[I Peter 3:15 "...always being ready to make a defense to everyone who asks you to give an account for the hope that is in you, yet with gentleness and reverence."]**

Feel free to write more than one skills statement, especially if you have more than one career area or if you are writing this résumé for a change in career area. After you complete this statement, you will write a theological statement to share your Christian beliefs.

❖ <u>List what you consider to be the top five most "marketable" skills, abilities, accomplishments, or areas of knowledge from the information you gathered in parts one and two of the assessment workshop.</u> What will the prospective church, organization or employer MOST need to know about what you know and can do? Compose descriptions in as few words as possible. Feel free to look ahead to the sample résumés to see how these statements may be applied. *Make every word count.*

    1.

    2.

    3.

    4.

    5.

❖ <u>List what you consider to be the top five most critical areas of doctrine that you wouldn't compromise for anybody or any position.</u> What will a church or missions organization MOST need to know about your spiritual life and commitment to the Lord that would make a difference in whether they call you or someone else? This can include points from your church's doctrinal statement, but should be personal and reflect YOU. *Make every word count.*

    1.

    2.

    3.

    4.

    5.

Identifying Your Specific Self-Management Skills

Now that you have mapped out your accomplishments and broader knowledge "base" in detail, it's time to identify the **more specific attributes** that enabled you to achieve your accomplishments. NEXT TO ALL words or phrases from the list below that you believe describe you, cite a brief example of how you have used this skill, ability, or attribute in the past. Be objective and don't be afraid to "brag" on yourself. There is a marked difference between arrogance and confidence! Treat this as a serious brainstorming activity. You will be pleased with the results. Clients of all ages and experience levels have over and over again expressed how much this activity has helped them "market" themselves to a prospective employer.

Able to meet deadlines

Able to prioritize

Articulate

Attentive to detail

Competent

Conscientious

Diligent

Efficient

Energetic

Excellent interpersonal skills

Fast learner

Flexible

Innovative

Persuasive

Positive

Problem solver

Productive

Professional

Punctual

Reliable

Resourceful

Responsible

Self-motivated

Versatile

Well organized

Work well as part of team

Work well independently

Work well under pressure

NOW – SUMMARIZE YOUR SKILLS
Crafting Your Summary Statement

The next step in being able to "market" yourself to a prospective employer is to combine your knowledge, accomplishments, basic skills, and self-management skills into a "useful tool". Using complete sentences, write a summary statement of no less than three paragraphs that describes YOU <u>as you would describe yourself to a prospective church, organization or employer</u> who wants to know who you are and what you can offer his or her company — why you should be hired. You should somehow incorporate the five "most marketable skills" you identified in the last part of this lesson. This statement will help in the writing of both your résumé and a cover letter. The next page is left intentionally blank if you wish to use it to hand write your statement. If you prefer, you may type it on your computer or hand write it on a separate piece of paper. You may wish to write more than one.

LOOKING AT IT FROM THE PERSPECTIVE OF THE EMPLOYER, EXPLAIN WHAT EXPERIENCES, SKILLS, KNOWLEDGE AND PERSONAL ATTRIBUTES YOU HAVE THAT WOULD COMPEL THIS PERSON TO HIRE YOU. KEEP IN MIND THAT THERE MIGHT BE 200-2,000 OTHER PEOPLE IN THIS "COMPETITION", YOU NEED TO STAND OUT FROM THE CROWD!

SKILLS STATEMENT:

Crafting Your Theological, Doctrinal, or "I Believe" Statement

The final step in this lesson is to write out a doctrinal, theological, or "I believe statement that can be included with your résumé and cover letter should it be requested (or should you believe it is in your best interest to include it). You should at least attempt to incorporate the five doctrinal/theological points you identified in the last part of this lesson. This statement will also help you be ready to answer questions regarding your beliefs and Christian walk. The rest of this page is left intentionally blank if you wish to use it to hand write your statement. If you prefer, you may type it on your computer or hand write it on a separate piece of paper.

CAREER OR JOB OBJECTIVE & ANALYSIS OF SKILLS

As with the previous section, I have included this activity because I have found it over the years to be critical to the writing of a good résumé and preparing my clients to confidently advance into the interview process. Please be serious about it. You will be very glad you did as you prepare to take the next step in your Christian service or career – or adapt to a new one! Some of these exercises may seem redundant, but they really do complement and "cement" each other; and it is impossible for you to be too well prepared to write your résumé!

CAREER OR JOB OBJECTIVE

Write a brief, concise statement (no more than 3 sentences) of your intent in pursuing this particular call/position/career in relation to what you can offer a church, organization or employer. In most, but not all, cases, I don't "waste space" on a résumé with an objective. I include this part of the activity more for you to be clear on what your purpose is in writing this résumé. You may or may not ultimately include it on your résumé. Ninety percent of the time, I would recommend you do NOT include an "objective" on your résumé.

Do any of the following apply to you in the work you do now or have done in the past? [Students, please apply these to your school experiences] Next to each item that applies to your individual situation, briefly explain any specifics that demonstrate these skills in your previous experience, whether it be from a job, community service, volunteer position, etc. Be honest in assessing your abilities.

Skills Analysis Part One:

Leadership Ability

Teaching Ability

Self-Discipline

Critical Thinking

Perseverance

Research Techniques

Cultural Perspective

Writing

Imagination

Which two of these qualities have you used most in the past?

Which two would you like to increase?

Why?

Skills Analysis Part Two: At the end of any statement that applies to you, write a brief explanation of the specifics of that experience. Bear in mind that if you have been in full-time ministry or missions for a long time, many of these will not be applicable to you. Use those that are pertinent to your own experiences.

Did you launch a new ministry or mission opportunity? If yes, describe in detail:

Did you train anyone ? (even as a volunteer). How many? How often?

Did you volunteer to assume responsibilities that weren't originally part of your job?

Were you promoted rapidly or rewarded generously?

Did you save money for your church, or organization or company?

Did you introduce new or more effective techniques for increasing productivity in your department or company?

Did you make a suggestion for or help launch a new product or program?

If your responsibilities included sales, did you increase sales on your own or assist someone else in increasing sales?

Did your employer create a new job slot for you?

Did you generate new business, bring in new clients or seek out/create affiliations with other organizations?

Did you design or institute any new system or process?

Did you meet an impossible deadline through extra effort on your part or as a result of your team efforts?

Did you rescue or turn around a project, transforming it from a failure to a success?

Did you alert your company/supervisor to a potential problem or a major opportunity?

Did you bring a major project in under budget?

Are there any other areas of knowledge or skill you believe will be a factor in getting an interview for this call or opportunity?

SECTION TWO

❧❧

THE
RÉSUMÉ
WRITING
WORKSHOP

RÉSUMÉ WRITING COURSE

We've had our "entrees", now we're ready to get to the "meat" of this course. Please note that you CANNOT complete this study course to the best of your ability unless you COMPLETE the previous section of skills assessment activities, READ and STUDY the Résumé "Crash Course", and carefully follow the directions as you go through the Résumé Information WorkSheet.

The rest of the exercises in this section will walk you through completion of a résumé that is "just right for you". You will learn the basics of résumé writing and gather information necessary to write the best possible résumé based on your CURRENT education and experience.

<u>This is not intended to be a hypothetical exercise, although you may "play" with future possibilities if you so choose</u>. This section of the study course includes a complete "crash course" on résumé writing, a brief series of questions on résumé writing to "cement" your knowledge, and an information-gathering form. The actual "crash course" is a prerequisite to the Résumé Writing Assignment you will be doing in the next part of the study course.

A. Read and study the "Résumé Crash Course" <u>thoroughly</u>. It is recommended that you read it through at least twice before answering the questions and beginning the worksheet.

B. Study the verb sheet.

C. Answer the questions using the information provided in the "Résumé Crash Course".

D. Review your "Skills and Abilities" worksheets from the previous study course section.

E. Complete all areas of the Résumé Information WorkSheet. Be thorough — this is a serious brainstorming session. <u>How well your résumé turns out will be a direct result of how much effort and thought you put into this process</u>.

Welcome to the "Crash Course"

When I was first asked by a college professor acquaintance to prepare a classroom presentation on résumé writing for a college English class in the mid 1990s, I had a terrible time squeezing "everything I knew" into a 90-minute block of time. Over the years, I have refined and condensed my classroom presentation and have come up with what I consider to be a pretty "efficient" 90 minutes of intense learning. This is where the "crash course" part came into the story.

> In today's micro-managed, technologically advanced job market there is an increasing need to have your résumé be as concise as possible. The "standard" for Christian résumés is no different.

Some of the community schools "classes" I've done have been as short as 30 minutes, which is <u>really</u> stretching it as far as covering the information needed to effectively teach résumé writing. Most of my workshops in recent years have been three consecutive one-hour sessions. This "crash course" is a condensed version of the condensed version, so to speak.

My advice to you is to completely read through the "Crash Course" and Information Gathering sections before you write down a single thing on paper. You may, of course, go through it any way you wish – you bought it, it is yours to do with as you please.

As I'm sure you've noticed, each element of this book concludes with a review to help "cement" what you've learned and a space for any notations you may wish to make. It is my desire that you glean the most possible information from the book. God gave me the knowledge to share, so I'm sharing it!

<u>"My Card … "</u>

Your résumé is, in effect, your "calling card". It may be THE most important document you "own" in your life. What it needs to be is a one- to two-page advertising campaign designed to *sell your assets* (experience, skills, knowledge, theology, and education) and <u>persuade a prospective church, organization, or employer to go to the next step and meet you in person</u>. That's all a résumé is — a process by which to gain an interview. Plain and simple. Too many people try to make it more than it is!

One of the worst mistakes people make is treating their résumé as if it's an untamable monster rather than considering it as their "new best friend". YOU, yes YOU, can write a "professional" résumé with just a little help. And if (Heaven forbid) you decide for some reason you are still not up to the task, you will be infinitely more prepared to take your résumé to someone else to finish for you (perhaps even to me). I periodically assist a "crash course" client in finishing up his or her résumé under the umbrella of my "Review/Critique" fee. See http://www.wordcopro.com for details if you're interested.

Concise Writing

A résumé is truly an exercise in *concise writing*. Although you'll hear some folks say, "Oh a résumé is easy — it's just an outline of your experience and education, I've done lots of those," it's not as easy as you might think; and it's entirely possible they've never actually done one (or at least a GOOD one!). If you've ever tried, you probably already know this is true.

When I present my résumé-writing workshop in a college class, it is presented as just that — an exercise in concise writing. It makes a natural addition to a college English class — teaching concise writing skills in a useful and practical way.

In today's micro-managed, technologically advanced job market there is an increasing need to have your résumé be as concise as possible. This is no different for Christian résumés. Some employers require a résumé to be no more than one page and "scanable", which necessitates giving extra-special attention to making every word count and laying your information out in a format in which a scanner can pick it up without garbling the characters and making it partially — or sometimes completely — unreadable.

Perhaps you already have an acceptable résumé in your file drawer or computer hard drive but you think it could use some improvement in one way or another. There are few résumés, including mine, that can't use a little improvement from time to time. If you like your current résumé, but need a "tune-up", you will find information here that will help you.

Resources Available To You

Most of the résumé writing books available on the market today are geared to "white-collar" jobs. They have cute, catchy titles and some of them have very good information in them; but they often leave out whole sections of the job market.

Virtually none of them have a clue what it takes to write a résumé for someone called to missions or ministry. This includes pastors, associate pastors, youth pastors, music ministers, music directors, worship leaders, missions directors, missionaries, other missions general personnel (pilots, maintenance workers, translators, etc.), and others.

And many don't include information and samples necessary to write an appropriate résumé for trade or industrial positions, such as union laborers, instrument technicians and equipment operators; for loggers, miners, waitresses, housekeepers and grocery clerks; for those in the military (or preparing to leave the military for the private sector) or a for myriad of others in today's work force who need specifically-targeted résumés.

Once upon a time employees in many of these categories (as well as many others) didn't even NEED a résumé — they just applied directly. This is no longer true, and today's authors need to (but often don't) reflect this in their résumé "how to" texts. In addition, there are actually many companies today that use a résumé *in lieu of an application and do not use the application process at all*. This makes having a well-written résumé even more important to you!

> … huge layoffs in recent years have created a glut of job-seekers in certain professions, and your résumé absolutely HAS to demonstrate what makes you "stand out in a crowd". Although our focus is generally different, Christian workers are not always completely exempt from this issue.

And even for "white-collar" employees, huge layoffs in recent years have created a glut of job-seekers in certain professions, and your résumé absolutely HAS to demonstrate what makes you "stand out in a crowd". This increases the need for newer, better résumé writing techniques and methods. Christian workers are not exempt from "mass layoffs". Tithing can be hit hard by job losses or decreasing business revenue, and churches and ministries can suffer financially in an economic downturn.

Although what you will read here summarizes more than two decades of studying about and writing résumés, I won't be offended if you look elsewhere for information as well. There are almost always pointers you can pick up from *any* book on résumés, old or new; and in my opinion, you can't know too much about résumé writing in today's tough job markets. *The more you know*, the better prepared you will be to organize and write a truly useful résumé — one that will get you results. Don't expect to find very many that deal with résumé writing from a Christian perspective, however.

More than a few of the résumé writing books in community libraries (as well as college libraries) are very much outdated, so be aware and watchful. One of the premier information sources for résumé writing (for me as well as for you) is current business-related magazines (look up résumé articles in their electronic periodical catalog if they have one).

Often current periodicals (like *Time, Newsweek, U. S. News & World Report,* etc.) will have articles on résumé writing that are usually up to date. Don't overlook the Internet as a potential source of information, either (after all, that's probably where you found ME!) You likely already know that any of the commonly used search engines will come up with several thousand possibilities when you search the terms "résumé writing" or "résumé tips" – and even "Christian résumé writer".

A word of CAUTION: Many typists for hire, *although they may have excellent typing skills*, do not have adequate knowledge of **résumé writing** to assist you in choosing either an appropriate format or what to write, especially when it comes to résumé writing from a Christian perspective.

Not all résumé writing information you come up with in a search will be CORRECT, however. So pray for wisdom in determining if a source is actually going to be helpful.

If you have questions, you can always email me at ceo@wordcopro.com for clarification. Make sure the "subject line" says YRACC2 Client Question", so I recognize the message as from someone who has purchased the book and is looking for help.

The Other Side of the Coin

Most of you can bypass this section. There is little "demand" for Christian workers in government positions. If you're a Christian who has been led of the Lord to apply for a secular position with the government, however, you may find the information useful.

For the most part, government agencies want details and details and more details in the job information they ask for from you; but virtually all other employers want to see brief, to-the-point statements of fact that clearly declare what you know and what you have to offer.

Filling out government applications is such a different "technical" skill that some government entities periodically give *classes* on writing out every intricate detail of your work history for their positions. If you are considering applying with one of these agencies, I suggest you take one of the courses if they're offered near you — it's virtually the ONLY way you can get enough "points" to get on the list unless you have a personal acquaintance or co-worker who is very familiar with the process on whom you can rely for advice. There are also books available on the subject.

Government applications are always a special challenge for me — my trade is _concise_ writing; and expounding on every detail; e.g. picked up the envelope, opened it, removed the contents, assessed the contents, logged the contents, dispatched the contents to the appropriate party or file, picked up the next envelope ... does not come naturally to me. I dislike it so much, in fact, that I usually charge double for typing government applications!

Today's government "work experience" summary should thoroughly describe every aspect of each position and be done in a simple font without bullet points, italics, or bold-face type so that it can be run through their scanning software without coming out a mess.

Please take the time to investigate a particular government agency where you are considering applying – their policies and practices aren't always in line with Christian values.

Not All Résumés Are Created Equal

The majority of the résumés I wrote for Alaskans in the 10 years I was in business there were petrochemical or other industrial employees who needed a completely different type of résumé than those found in any of the two dozen books on the subject I had read at the time. I found I had to quickly stretch and grow in my abilities as a résumé writer. Many of the oil companies (and the school district as well) sent numerous people to me upon seeing my work, so I obviously was doing something right!

Because my online service is advertised as a "Christian" résumé service, I have had many ministry and missions clients over the years. It has been a blessing to be of service to God's people answering His call on their lives.

A word of CAUTION: Many typists for hire, *although they may have excellent typing skills*, do not have adequate knowledge of **résumé writing** to assist you in choosing either an appropriate format or what to write, especially when it comes to résumé writing from a Christian perspective. There are two basic formats I use, with several variations of each, depending upon the type of work you do, how long you've been doing it, how long you've been working altogether, and what sort of business or organization will be receiving the résumé.

Even if you write your own résumé and you hire a typist to get it on paper for you, make sure that YOU *carefully proofread* it, or have someone you trust proofread it. The more the merrier! For purposes of updating and flexibility in applying for multiple positions, doing your résumé on a computer is highly desirable.

And please, please, PLEASE! If you end up taking your résumé to a typist, do not accept shoddy work at any price or for any reason. If your résumé isn't done to your satisfaction, insist that they do it over again, regardless of how much or how little they are charging you for the work.

The pages that follow are, I believe, as concise and complete a résumé "quick study" as currently exists. This information covers all of the most important points necessary for you to understand to succeed at writing a résumé tailored to your specific needs and wants. There is no need for you to read volumes of information to write a great résumé. If you have specific questions when you have finished the course, you are welcome to email me for additional information.

No matter whether your format ends up being formal, cute, artsy, or stark (These days most experts advise simplicity, because so many companies run résumés through a scanner and then software that scans for key words), it's the WORDS on it that will make the difference. A great-looking format isn't worth the paper it is printed on if it doesn't get them to CALL you for an interview!

It is generally acceptable, and often desirable, for a pastor and wife or missionary couple to include a photograph in one of the upper corners of the résumé. It should be small enough to not "hog" space, but big enough to be worth having on the page.

"... who has saved us and called us with a holy calling, not according to our works, but according to His own purpose and grace which was granted us in Christ Jesus from all eternity." – II Timothy 1:9

Ok, Let's Get Down To The Nitty Gritty
(This is the actual "crash course")

> *Whatever your area of expertise, job goal/career goal, experience, or education, there are consistent elements to a résumé that employers will notice and reward with a phone call:*

What Format Do I Use?

1.1   As I mentioned in the introduction, there are only two basic formats I have used the last 22+ years for résumé writing. Both involve reverse chronological listings of employment and experience (education is always listed in reverse chronological order, as well). One format begins with a bulleted qualifications summary and has a very different "look" to it. The other has a brief, usually one-sentence summary of qualifications, followed by as many detailed job description entries as are pertinent to the position you are targeting.

Variations of these two formats are appropriate for virtually any modern résumé. I almost never use what most résumé books call a "functional" résumé which does not include any dated job listings at all. There are specific, very limited occasions when such a résumé is appropriate; however, most of the time when I see a truly "functional" résumé format, I always wonder what the writer is "hiding". See Samples.

1.2   **Rule #1. Write and design for readability**. The résumés I have written over the years *all have one thing in common* ... a term that I call "**scanability**©". My résumés are purposefully and carefully designed in such a way that an employer can very rapidly eye-scan the text for pertinent information, then presumably (if you've done your job right, the word is <u>assuredly</u>) be interested enough to go back and read it through in depth. *Rule #2. There is no need for further rules if you follow Rule #1.*

Not All Résumés Are Created Equal

This term "scanability©" I use here is not the same concept as having a résumé formatted to be placed in a computer scanner and scanned for key words or scanned into a company's files. My use of the term "scanability"© specifically has to do with what the human eye (and ultimately the human brain) can and will pick up in a glance involving just a few seconds' time span. The ability (gift or knack, if you will) to write and design résumés in this way is one of the main factors that keeps clients coming to me year after year.

1.3   I'm going to repeat this point because it is probably *THE* most important overall aspect of your résumé. The person reading your résumé *MUST* be able to quickly eye-scan it for *pertinent* information. Priority items should absolutely *LEAP* out at the reader for observation. ***This is a competition!*** Treat it as such. I can't emphasize it too much — you have to get and keep the reader's attention in three seconds or less! Job seekers need an "edge" in today's market and this is the best one available. Take advantage of it while you can!

1.4   In basic formatting aspects, the Christian worker's résumé won't differ fundamentally from a secular résumé. For a music minister or missionary, there is a little more room for "artsy" additions to a résumé, but I still generally advise clients to keep it conservative. This is the "better safe than sorry" concept.

1.5   Although a lot of people still insist on using it, the old "Harvard Business School" format is space consuming and (in my humble opinion) plays too heavily on dates for many people. The Harvard Business School format is not "eye-scanable" by any stretch of the imagination. For those who insist on using this format, try to use bold or italic type, capitals or underlines to accent your position and key words that highlight your experience. (If you believe it will NOT be run through a scanner).

For those with only one or two jobs to document at which you spent considerable time, it is certainly not unacceptable, though never my first choice for an appropriate format. With the exception of a couple of entertainers, I have not designed a résumé on the old style format for a client for nearly 20 years. There are much better ways to "display your wares".

1.6   The manner in which you list job start and end dates on your résumé can work either for you or against you, depending on how long your time of service was in the positions you will be listing. For many of my Alaska résumé clients, dates were the *last thing* they wanted the employer to focus on — most roustabouts, crane operators, wireline hands, welders, fitters, equipment operators, etc. according to "the nature of the beast", in that area worked many jobs for many employers (they have to go where the work is). The focus most certainly needed to be **on experience, NOT on dates**. It wasn't at all a matter of the employee being irresponsible, unreliable or "jumping around" from job to job. It's just the way the job market was (and still is in many places worldwide).

Many people in ministry, especially those just entering full-time ministry, have been attending college for a good number of years and may have part-time and/or volunteer positions in various capacities in ministry. Sometimes education has been stretched out over many years to avoid accumulating any debt in the process.

> Remember, your objective with this résumé is to generate enough interest in a prospective church board, mission organization, or other employer that he or she will call you to set up an interview appointment.

This same point applies to many union laborers. A 25-year union electrician or equipment operator has worked hundreds of projects for dozens of employers and can't *possibly* LIST all of them. In this case, the wise résumé writer *broadly summarizes experience and knowledge*, then highlights large or otherwise *noteworthy* projects and essential skills and training. See Samples.

Based on how you see your experience from the prospective employer's viewpoint, you will have to use your judgment on how to list start and end dates on your résumé. If you have had a number of jobs in a short time, no matter what the reason, you will most likely want to underplay dates and emphasize experience. If you have had only a couple of jobs that lasted for years and you moved up through the ranks, steadily increasing your skills and knowledge, or if you worked for churches, organizations, or companies with very prestigious name recognition, that will influence your choice of format. If church, organization, or company names recognized in your industry or occupation will make a difference in whether they call you for an interview, make sure you place those on the left where they will be seen right away.

Remember, your objective with this résumé is to generate enough interest in a prospective church board, missions organization, or other employer that you will receive a phone call to set up an interview appointment. It is not deceptive or underhanded to state facts in such a way that the reader will initially pick up the information you most want him or her to know.

1.7   Virtually all résumés should be organized *chronologically*, beginning with your most recent experience. Even if you are a recent high school or college graduate with little relevant experience, I recommend putting your education/training last; however, important degrees/courses should be *highlighted in the qualifications summary* at the beginning of the résumé.

I seldom put the "Education" category first unless the client feels very strongly about it. In the "old school", teachers almost always listed education first, and it is an acceptable personal choice to do so now. Given the choice, if a person has a pertinent degree, especially with educators and business execs, I list it in a *prominent* place in the qualifications summary, then repeat it briefly in the "Education" section near the end of the résumé. This may seem redundant, but it is acceptable and advisable in my opinion. If you have "Dr." in front of your name, you should include it in your name heading at the top of the résumé.

1.8   It is incredibly difficult to *document* some jobs (including many industrial and trade positions). My oldest brother, for instance, when he was a camp maintenance foreman at Alaska's Kuparuk oil field, worked for three different employers in three years in the <u>same job</u>. *Each year the plant maintenance contract for services provided was awarded to a different contractor through a bidding process*, but my brother was hired to continue in his same job by each new contract company. His résumé lists that block of time as **one** "job", with a brief notation at the end of the summary paragraph explaining the change in contractors. To do otherwise would have consumed unnecessary space and created *unwanted confusion*. I have never personally seen any other résumé writer make use of this space-(and confusion) saving option. It works wonders for non-typical job entries of this type.

> You have to see yourself through the eyes of the person you plan to be working for next!

> If you have had a number of jobs in a short time, no matter what the reason, you will most likely want to underplay dates and emphasize experience.

This concept also applies if you worked for one church, organization or company in continually advancing or vastly different positions. They should be listed under the heading of a single "employer", but set apart for review. The "Martin Missionary" résumé sample displays this technique in one of the job description entries. It is also possible to identify advancing positions within a company or organization by writing it into the descriptive paragraph.

Another client, during her four college years, worked in a number of primarily summer positions "jumping back and forth" between the Department of Natural Resources and the U. S. Forest Service — and they were all relevant to her career. It was a special challenge to list those positions in a manner that effectively conveyed what the prospective employer needed to know without taking up half of the available space on the résumé.

1.9   Review the rest of the résumés in the Samples section for complete "eye-witness" information on how to lay out a concise, highly readable reverse chronological résumé. I don't know if you're a visual learner like I am, but I can "*show*" you some things a lot more easily than I can "*tell*" you. The techniques used in these résumés can be applied to almost any résumé. Feel free to combine the techniques in your personal résumé.

1.10 If you find that your résumé will not quite fit on the number of pages you have decided are appropriate, you can sometimes change margins to .9 rather than 1.0, or even to .85 or .80. Virtually no one will notice this change on the printed page.

You can also change paragraph spacing to .9 or .8 in between paragraphs — or even .5 between items that don't have to have lots of "white space". Changing 10 spaces to .9 (or two to .5) will give you a whole line if you're just one line short of fitting on the page. The space above this paragraph is .8. The space below it is 1.0.

What Do I Say and How Do I Say It?

2.1 The most important point of this section is that you must focus on what your "audience" will want to know about your skills and experience. IF YOU DON'T GET ANYTHING ELSE OUT OF THIS SECTION, GET THIS – YOU HAVE TO SEE YOURSELF THROUGH THE EYES OF THE PERSON YOU PLAN TO BE WORKING FOR NEXT! THIS IS NO DIFFERENT FOR CHRISTIAN WORKERS!

If YOU were calling or hiring someone for this position, what would you most want to know about that person? The old "walk a mile in my shoes" philosophy works very well here and I highly recommend it. Your résumé can't be its best if you don't **seriously adopt this viewpoint**.

2.2 Stop right now for a few moments and *imagine* yourself as your potential deacon/elder board, pastor search committee, supervisor or employer. Get out pen and paper and make a list of what *key skills or abilities* this person or body is going to want to see in the individual hired for the job or call you're applying for (or the job you plan to go after next).

Please note this very important point -- *If you don't have exact matches* on the specific qualifications that are being requested in an advertisement or posting, determine what experience, skills or education/training you **DO** have that will *most closely match* the stated requirements. This is one of the reasons I have placed so much emphasis on having you thoroughly assess your skills, abilities and knowledge. It is also a reason to write a detailed cover letter, which is covered later in this study course.

2.3   In today's high-tech job market (*including McDonald's*), you should be sure to highlight ANY *computer* or *keyboarding* experience you have. It can actually make the difference between getting or not getting that interview over someone else who has similar qualifications but has no (or has not <u>listed</u>) computer experience at all. If you at *least* know how to turn a computer on and find your way around the "desktop", it is to your advantage. <u>Be *careful* with your word usage though, so you don't overstate your skill level.</u> Don't say "*experienced*" if you are only "*familiar*" with particular hardware or software applications. If you have very limited experience, you might use the phrase "computer literate". PLEASE !! <u>Don't "fudge" on this! A new employer will be able to tell right away on the job if you *weren't quite truthful* on this point</u>.

> To be "safe", it is advisable for you to do a "test scan" of your résumé if you are creating it to be scanned, faxed, or otherwise input via electronic media.

How explicit you get about your computer experience will be somewhat determined by the *type of position* for which you are applying. Don't assume that computer skills won't be desirable or used, though, just because you're answering a call to ministry or missions. A pastor, associate pastor, youth pastor, or music director may very well be called upon to create, or at least operate, video presentations in applications such as PowerPoint®.

In addition, many, many jobs today (including industrial and trade positions) require computer knowledge for computerized *control* and *monitoring* equipment, *inventory* management, scheduled and unscheduled *maintenance* tracking, project *estimating/bidding*, and *shipping/receiving* just to name a few. And if you've been to the grocery store or fast food restaurant lately, you are perfectly well aware that *technology* is truly EVERYWHERE! Briefly state what you believe the prospective employer will want to know about your computer hardware and/or software experience, either in the qualifications summary or in individual job description paragraphs — or both — as appropriate for you.

2.4   So how much *detail* SHOULD you provide for each separate entry? That's a difficult question to answer, depending on your chosen career field and the type of job for which you are applying. If there's anything I've discovered in 22+ years of résumé writing, it is that EACH résumé is different.

Unless you are changing career fields or applying for a job outside your area of normal expertise, in the majority of situations, deacon/elder boards and pastor search committees (or personnel department heads in a secular field) will have a thorough knowledge of your ministry area and can make certain *assumptions* just from as few words as a position and employer. This is not always true, however. In most cases, *less is better*. The person reading your résumé doesn't want to read a "*book*". You want to give just enough information to get you called in for an interview. Then you can tell him, her or them ALL about yourself face to face. Ideally, when you are finished with your new résumé, there will be just enough detail to *set you apart from the "crowd"* but not bore the reader or "turn him or her off".

2.5   Once again, put yourself in the interviewer's place. If the position for which you are submitting the résumé is *within* your field of expertise, you will not have to include nearly as much detail as you will if the position is a *career change* or something *outside* of the specific area(s) in which you have previously been employed or schooled. Use common sense here. Just for an example, the owner of a retail tire store isn't likely to be able to make assumptions about all the responsibilities you had as the manager of a ski rental shop. On each individual job description entry on the résumé, ask yourself this question: Is the person reading my résumé going to understand what a certain position entailed if I don't give adequate detail?

Ministry and missions calls can have very different responsibilities, depending on what the rest of the ministry or missions "team" looks like.

Be sure to add just enough detail to encourage them to call you for an interview.

2.6   How *long* should your résumé be? There are those who continue to insist that a résumé must be only *ONE* page. One page is certainly ideal, IF you can get all the pertinent information on it. However, NEVER use tiny fonts or leave out important information to keep it on one page! The "norm" is *two pages* in most instances today. I have spent more than just a little time "picking the brains" of supervisors who do a LOT of hiring, and have had *most* of them agree that they don't care how long a résumé is as long as it contains all **_relevant_** information. The key word here, of course, is *relevant*. "Just the facts" is a good rule of thumb.

2.7   Today's job market – and that includes Christian workers in ministry and missions – sometimes requires résumés to be ONLY one-page and set up to put into a computer scanner and scanned into a database or other files. Keep in mind that you need to use "clean" fonts (avoid dramatic serifs and condensed fonts) and simple formatting so that the scanner won't garble the information and render your wonderful résumé unreadable. My favorite fonts for this are Verdana 11 (much of this book is in Verdana 10, which is almost too small for most résumés), Tahoma 11 or 12 and Zurich Ex BT 11. Generally a <u>job posting will indicate if the résumé is to be limited to one page</u> and formatted for scanning. Most of my résumé formatting techniques end up being suitable for scanning. In general, modern scanners don't have too much of a problem with standard bullet lists and simple fonts.

To be "safe", it is advisable for you to do a "test scan" of your résumé if you are creating it to be scanned, faxed, or otherwise input via electronic media. Then you'll know how the format and fonts respond and whether the end result will be attractive and useful. I would suggest that you scan it and email it to a friend, relative, or co-worker; as well as faxing it to someone as a test. Converting to .pdf is also an option.

A "mega-church" will, of course, be more likely to run your résumé through scanning software than a rural church with 100 members.

2.8   Although you may not choose to include them all on your résumé, I recommend listing out *every* job you've *ever* had on the outline form so that you can adequately *summarize* your experience. You may only end up putting the last four or five actual jobs you've had (or one or two if you've been at them for many years), then *summarize* the rest of your work history in one or two brief one-sentence entries or even in one entry in the qualifications summary or at the end of the experience section of your résumé. As long as you have space available, there is nothing wrong with including generalized summary blocks of time at the end of the résumé to account for time spent and noteworthy experience gained. If you say you have 20 years of experience, but they are only seeing 10, the reader may question your honesty.

If you are writing a résumé for a ministry or missions call but have work experience that is totally unrelated to ministry or missions, you may wish to include a brief summary of "one-liners" documenting where you were and what you were doing over the previous years before you went into ministry (or jobs you held because your ministry salary was not full-time pay). You will have to use your judgment to determine whether such experience should be included or excluded. It is fairly common to include an experience section titled "Additional Experience". Martin Missionary's sample résumé simply states at the end that he has 10 years of experience in construction management.

2.9   If you have been a supervisor but *don't* want to be one again, briefly state, but *underplay*, any supervisory experience or *leave* it off entirely. Sometimes a person has served in a supervisory capacity to find they *dislike* it intensely and do not wish to do it again if it can be avoided. If you WANT to be a supervisor, but have little supervisory experience, be sure to *prominently* list any supervisory experience you have — even if it was at VBS or on the baseball team (provided you have space available without making your résumé overlong).

2.10   If you want to *continue* as — or *desire to be* — a supervisor, a one-sentence summary of any supervisory experience should definitely appear in the <u>qualifications summary</u> at the beginning of your résumé. Make sure you *quantify* your previous supervisory experience, if you have any. *How many* employees did you supervise? Did you *train* any of them yourself? Did you set up their *work schedules*?

2.11   Each job description paragraph should *begin* with those duties or responsibilities that are *MOST* important to the reader to know, prioritizing your way through the rest of the paragraph, ending with the least important duties/responsibilities. You may have to *rewrite* these several times to get your priorities in order; and they may, in fact, change from résumé to résumé depending on a particular position you are applying for. (You may wish to create more than one résumé if you are applying for multiple positions that will necessitate re-prioritizing your key responsibilities more than a time or two).

Highlighting key words with **bold type** or *italics* or even ***bold italics*** can be very effective if all of the information in a paragraph is equally important. See "John Mortgage Lender" sample résumé. Just remember that simple is better, and <u>overuse of specialty typestyles can be a detriment rather than a benefit to the reception your résumé will receive from the reader</u>. It also makes the résumé more difficult to electronically scan.

Once again, remember to *prioritize the paragraph according to how a prospective employer would want to read it*. They may only read the first two or three words of the paragraph in their initial "scan", *make them count*!

2.12   Make sure you stay *consistent* grammatically. Just as an example, don't say "Responsibilities included typing, filing, answer telephone." The word should be "answering" to make the text flow.   Or say, "Typed, filed, answered phone." I know this may sound nitpicky; but in reality, *<u>anything that forces the reader </u>to slow down and "think"* reduces your *scanability*© effect and may lose you that interview opportunity. Watch your tense throughout EVERY paragraph and entry. Read it *out loud* to see how it "sounds", how it flows. Show your potential employer you care about grammar as well as spelling! Make your résumé FLOW! Of course, all previous jobs will list duties as past tense. Your current position (unless you are between jobs) will list duties in the present tense.

2.13   I *never* include salary history on a résumé, though there are some who do. In my professional opinion, including salary history on the résumé *takes up unnecessary space and reduces scanability©*. In most situations, your résumé will accompany a formal *application* on which your salary history is required. As with some other points, including or not including salary history is a *personal preference* and you have a choice to make. <u>Make note of any company requirements in an ad or posting</u>, because individual companies, organizations, and agencies have different requirements in this area.

If you know for sure that the résumé is requested in lieu of an application, you may choose to add salary history or create a *supplemental page* on the same paper and with the same format that lists your salary history and any other information you believe will be pertinent to getting you called in for an interview. It is always acceptable to call the pastor search committee, deacon/elder board, or human resources department and inquire what they prefer to receive from you (or require).

2.14   I almost never include the *reason for leaving a job*. Occasionally, when a company goes out of business or there are special circumstances a potential future employer should really know about, there are exceptions. This information will likely appear on an application and there is no need to duplicate it. If a job was *temporary*, especially a *very short-term* one, state it at the end of the description of duties. This is commonly used for summer positions held by high school and college students.

> I know this may sound nitpicky; but in reality, <u>*anything that forces the reader*</u> *to slow down and "think"* reduces your *scanability©* effect and may lose you that interview opportunity.

2.15   <u>Additional Note:</u> For an *Airline Hostess Résumé* — Some of the primary qualities important to airlines are professionalism, maturity, leadership ability, friendliness, concern for others, self-confidence, reliability, flexibility, thinking well "on your feet" and being a team player.

Do I Include a Job/Career Objective?

3.1   Many résumé books available today put what *I* consider to be way too much emphasis on "objective" — sometimes a CAREER objective, sometimes a JOB objective (which are not one and the same). I personally am not big on including either type of objective on your résumé, especially a "*generic*" one that sounds canned, like you *copied* it out of a book. If the first thing the reader sees is a phony sounding cut-and-pasted objective from a book, he or she may be too *turned off* to continue at all.

> I'm particularly fond of seeing a well-written qualifications summary as the first thing the reader sees on a résumé …

Don't get me wrong, I believe you should HAVE both a job and a career objective. I just don't agree that it should always *appear* on your résumé. If you are NOT sending a cover letter and you have adequate space without crowding the information, it can be a good idea to include a specific job objective if you are applying for a specific position with the résumé — especially if it's a large company.

3.2   For most of the hundreds of people for whom I've done résumés, a career objective was secondary. It is, in fact, possible for a career objective listed on your résumé to work <u>against</u> you — if the first thing the reader sees is your career objective to be the department head, *the department head reading your résumé* may feel threatened and toss your résumé into "File 13". In most cases, this is a matter of personal preference and you will have to give it some serious thought and prayer and decide for yourself. If you feel strongly about putting an objective on your résumé, then it's your choice to make.

3.3   It is perfectly acceptable to indicate the position for which you are applying as an "objective"; although if you don't have a computer on which you can easily change the objective for each résumé, it is probably best left to a simple *cover letter* to outline what position you are applying for and how your qualifications specifically fit in with their requirements. I would also take "space" on the résumé into consideration. If you have a nice, tight résumé and adding an objective at the top will push you onto another page or squeeze entries into too small a space, my personal and professional recommendation is to cut the objective. I'm particularly fond of seeing <u>a well-written qualifications summary as the first thing the reader sees</u> on a résumé — not an objective of any sort.

What About References?

4.1   Virtually all of the "experts" I've studied and consulted indicate that the words "References will be provided upon request" are best left off a résumé. Let's face it, your potential employer knows you'll provide references when asked, and that you're not going to give names of people who are going to say bad things about you — your references (along with everybody else's) are "stacked". There are certain things that can be assumed about a job applicant, and this is one of them. If people insist on having references on their résumé, I don't argue with them, however. I point out what I just "said" to you and let it go at that. This, too, is a matter of personal preference. After years of justifying my position on this issue, I am delighted to finally see today's "experts" advising people to *leave it off*!

4.2   I most commonly counsel clients to have four or five good, solid references listed on a separate sheet (on the same style paper as the résumé, same typestyle, same format; name at the top, e.g. "John Doe

> If there's anything I've discovered in 20+ years of résumé writing, it is that EACH résumé is different.

— Supplemental Information" as the header) that they carry to an interview to have available if requested by the interviewer (or to deliver or mail if it is requested once the prospective employer has your résumé in his or her hands). It is certainly your option. Carrying a short list of your best references to an interview is, in my opinion, a very good idea anyway. You never know if the interviewer will have all of the documentation you submitted with your application at hand at the time of your interview. Job postings sometimes request references.

Do I Need a Cover Letter?

5.1   Cover letters are always optional, but many times advisable. Different employers view cover letters very differently. I once entertained a summer guest (the head of a personnel department in California's Silicon Valley) who told me she *always* reads the cover letter *last, if at all*. Other employers, however, like to see a well-written cover letter tying your experience and education point by point into a particular position. *When in doubt*, go ahead and use one; but make sure it is specific, not "generic". A generic "send-it-out-to-anybody" cover letter is a waste of the reader's time. The only way to truly know for sure is to telephone the company and see if you can find somebody who will clue you in on the personal preference of the person who will be reading your résumé. In *most* cases, a brief cover letter will be more likely to help than to hurt as long as it doesn't sound like it's been directly copied from a book.

5.2   With today's tight job markets, I personally favor using cover letters — especially when you have more than one area of expertise or are changing career fields. A *concise* cover letter can point out to the employer *exactly* how your qualifications fit in with the requirements for a particular position. It is the *perfect* tool. This brings up another point — if you have a good description of the job for which you are applying, be sure to briefly highlight every point for which you qualify.

Note: If you have few direct qualifications for the position, be sure to point out specifically what other aspects of your education, training, and experience can substitute for those skills and abilities you lack. Highlight your ability to learn new tasks quickly and/or adapt to new situations rapidly (if you have that ability).

> I once entertained a summer guest (the head of a personnel department in California's Silicon Valley) who told me she *always* reads the cover letter *last, if at all*.

5.3   Cover letters should be *short* and to the point — three or four paragraphs, ideally. *Avoid* "flowery" language and going on and on with thank-yous. Keep it business-like and concise. I don't think I've ever done a cover letter that was more than one page. Name the position for which you are applying, if appropriate. If you are sending a résumé to be placed on file for a future opening, say so in the first paragraph. The next section of the study course briefly details cover letter writing techniques.

Miscellaneous Miscellany

6.1   Be sure to look over a *job application form* carefully BEFORE you begin filling it out. Many applications say right on them, usually somewhere near the top, that they are to be HAND WRITTEN, NOT TYPED. I can't tell you how many people I have had bring me applications to type which stated that requirement clearly right at the top of the form and I had to point it out to them. Sometimes they even specify the color of ink you are to use, so take a close look before starting.

6.2   **An IMPORTANT note on proofreading.** Every year my high school students hear from me, "The best way to proofread ANY document is to read it out loud to yourself or someone else to see how it "sounds". You will catch most spelling AND grammatical errors this way. You CANNOT rely on a spelling checker OR grammar checker to do the job for you. Spelling checkers will not catch errors such as "in" where you intended "on" — or "it" where it should be "at" or "hat" or "that". Grammar checkers will catch some of those basic errors, but cannot be relied upon solely. In my opinion, there is no better way than to print out your document and then read it aloud. You will have better results proofing a document in print in your hand than you will reviewing it on screen on the computer, as well. I can't tell you exactly why, but I know it to be true. This advice is based on nearly 30 years of proofreading documents, both for myself and for others. In an age of not wanting to "waste" paper, it is still advisable to print the document for the final proofread, in my opinion. If you truly feel led to save paper, then "zoom" in on your computer screen and view the document in as large a format as you can.

A Final Word of Advice

7.1   Most people don't think of themselves as a "product". According to established experts, in any given job search, you're going to be up against an unknown number of people, many of whom have skills as strong as (or even stronger than) yours. Even if sales is not your line of work (or your strong suit), you MUST sell the prospective employer on calling you for an interview, and then ultimately hiring you. Christian workers can sometimes have an advantage over another candidate because of a closer match in theology. Make sure you clearly state your core beliefs, either in your cover letter or in a separate belief statement. Yes, you trust God to open the door (or close it), but that should not keep you from doing your best to get that interview if you believe this is the direction He is leading you at this time.

7.2   I highly recommend that you read back through the "crash course" one more time before you complete the study sheet and continue to the information worksheet. Once that is accomplished, you are ready to begin the actual compilation of information to put on your résumé. Most likely, you already have an old résumé in a folder or envelope somewhere (or on your computer) and a few letters of reference stashed. You've probably just made some notes on recent experience. IF this is your first résumé, no problem.

7.3   Once you have completed the crash course "cement" questions on the next page, you will also need to review your "Skills and Abilities" worksheets.

Spelling checkers will not catch errors such as "in" where it should say "on" or "it" where it should say "at" or "hat" or "that".

Résumé Crash Course "CEMENT YOUR KNOWLEDGE" Worksheet

Answers should be based on the information provided in *Your Résumé: A Crash Course*

1.   Your résumé is designed to persuade a prospective employer to do what?

2.   A résumé is truly an exercise in _____ _____ .

3.   What is the basic rule on how long a résumé should be?

4.   Should you ever leave out important facts or use tiny fonts to keep your résumé on one page?

5.   Which direction do most people read?

6.   How should you see yourself when writing a résumé?

7.   The reader may only read how many words in each paragraph in the first scan?

8.   What should appear in the qualifications summary at the top of the résumé?

9.   How should a job description paragraph be prioritized?

10.   When might you need more than one résumé?

NOTES | NOTES | NOTES | NOTES

This space is provided for you to make notations on points you perceived to be important, questions you need answered, or a brainstorming session to "gel" what you want to see your résumé turn out like. If you have questions, feel free to email me at ceo@wordcopro.com.

Sample Résumés

This section includes a sampling of résumés for your review. These are representative of "treatments" done for various Christian worker occupations, ranging from a missionary to a pastor and a handful of résumés for secular positions for those who are writing the résumé from a Christian perspective, but not answering a call for ministry or missions service. I have included a résumé for a high school student for those home-school families who desire to provide instruction in résumé writing to their children.

I do not include dozens of samples as some books do, simply because there is no need for more than a handful of examples to give you the general picture I'm trying to convey. Your résumé should reflect YOU and should not be an exact imitation of any résumé from anybody's book (including mine). These samples demonstrate various ways to word responsibilities, as well as layouts that are easy on the eye and from which the pertinent information can be gleaned very quickly.

Résumés include:
- Peter Pastor (Th.D., extensive experience as pastor, director)
- Monte Missionary (MBA, missionary administrator, missionary pilot)
- Michael Music Minister (Bachelor's, working on Master's, limited paid music ministry experience, but solid volunteer experience and college education)
- Paul Youth Pastor (M. Ed., several youth ministry positions)
- Christian School Teacher/Athletic and Academic Coach (Certified K-12)
- Social Worker (B.S. working on Master's)
- Mortgage Lender (17+ years experience; Three pages by client's request)
- Full Charge Bookkeeper (A.A. Business Administration)
- Christian Singer/Musician (or Actor/Actress)
- High School Student ("Typical" high school student)

> … how I write résumés is based on proven results over the long term.

These ten résumés, combined, demonstrate all of the attributes I believe are essential to good résumé writing. Ideally, your résumé will be a combination of what you perceive as the best aspects of all of them, based on the knowledge you have gained through this process. You will note that the résumé of the mortgage lender is three pages and includes personal information. The length and the inclusion of personal info were the client's choice, not mine.

Opinions of résumé professionals vary GREATLY in this day and age, and you will likely find those who would advise you otherwise. You are certainly welcome to follow any advice you deem valuable. Keep in mind, however, that _how I write résumés is based on proven results over the long term_.

You will note that company names, individual names and locations have been altered "to protect the innocent". Please forgive the resulting redundancy. _I have reduced font sizes and altered spacing in some cases to make the documents fit in this book, which is smaller than the normal 8 ½ x 11" letter-sized paper you will use._ You will NOT want to use fonts this small for your résumé. Some minor aspects of formatting may not convert "cleanly" to the manuscript .pdf for my publisher, as well. You can get the general idea, however.

NOTE how few words are used to convey information. NO full sentences. NO use of the word "I". Consistent tense — past tense for previous jobs, present tense for current position (if applicable).

Each sample is followed by an explanation of the general qualities of the formatting and wording, along with an area where you may express what you like and dislike about it.

The next 20 pages contain samples and explanations. After you have scanned through them and made note of the qualities you like and/or believe will work best for you, you will want to complete your worksheets and get on with the process of actually writing your résumé.

Peter I. Pastor, Th.D.

000 Holy Spirit Dr. | Anytown, US 11333
555-555-1212 (Cell) | 555-555-1313 (Home)
ppastorthd@churchemail.org

SUMMARY OF QUALIFICATIONS

* Licensed and ordained pastor, passionate about teaching the Word of God to encourage and equip Believers to follow the Holy Spirit's leading to do the will and work of Christ
* Doctor of Theology
* Master of Christian Counseling
* Board certified faith-based clinical counselor since 2002
* Patient, compassionate listener with a genuine love for God's people
* Gifted in the area of seeing potential problems before they arise and analyzing situations for the best way to proceed
* Solid leadership and managerial skills
* Experienced with most computer software, including Internet website design software

SUMMARY OF MINISTRY EXPERIENCE

Founder/Director | *Online Ministry* | Current
* Serving the Lord using Biblical teaching and other resources to equip, educate, encourage, and empower believers (both individuals and churches) to become all God created them to be, and to do all God created them to do

Education Director | *Calvary Chapel* | Current
* Provide oversight of all education and discipleship

Pastor | *Hope Fellowship* | Anytown, US | July 2003 to July 2005
* Called to serve the Lord preaching, teaching, counseling, educating and leading
* Responsible for Sunday morning services and Wednesday evening Bible studies
* Served as worship leader as needed

Director | *Hope Christian Counseling Center* | Anytown, US | January 2003 to July 2003
* Responsible for the day-to-day operation of the clinic; counseling with clients, serving as case manager, answering phone, making appointments, handling marketing and advertising [ministry of Hope Fellowship]

Team Pastor | *Christ the Rock Outreach Ministry* | 1999 to 2002
* Responsible for spiritual leadership, guidance, counseling, preaching and education for evangelistic ministry incorporating drama, music and preaching to proclaim the Gospel

Pastor | *Christ the Rock Christian Fellowship* | Kerrville, Texas | 1999 to 2001
* Called to serve the Lord preaching, teaching, counseling, educating and leading
* Responsible for Sunday morning services and Wednesday evening Bible studies
* Served as worship leader as needed

Various | June 1996 to 2003
* Served the Lord in several part-time and full-time opportunities, including missions, street ministry, pastor, pulpit supply, evangelism, etc.

Peter I. Pastor | Page 1 of 2

Volunteer Church Ministries | 1990 to 1996 | Including, but not limited to:

- Served as **pulpit supply** preacher
- **Planned** and **organized** ministry teams, planned and organized church seminars, **provided oversight** of ministries such as hospital visitation, divorce recovery, grounds ministry, etc.
- In the area of hospital ministry, **provided worship service** (preaching and singing) for Anytown State Hospital residents
- Worked with ministry leaders to **coordinate** activities and church goals
- As youth and adult Bible study teacher, **prepared** and **taught** Wednesday and Sunday Bible studies for youth and adults
- Worked with other parents to provide Wednesday evening **youth services** and general **youth ministry activities**
- As Men's Ministry President, **coordinated** ministry activities, **arranged** monthly breakfast, provided Bible study or guest speaker for monthly breakfast
- Filled in for **worship leader** as needed

SUMMARY OF ADDITIONAL EXPERIENCE
Anytown, US

Current – Self-Employed
- Freelance Photographer [portrait and event photography]

1980 to 2003 Periodic, Depending on College Schedule
- Opthalmic Technician/Optician

EDUCATION AND SPECIALIZED TRAINING

Doctor of Theology | *Christian College and Seminary* | 2007
Master of Christian Counseling | *Christian College and Seminary* | 2003
Board Certified Faith-Based Clinical Counselor | *Institute of Faith Based Counseling* | 2002
Bachelor of Biblical Counseling | *Christian College and Seminary* | 2001

Various courses in Opticianry | 1980-1996
Graduate | Community High School | Anytown, US | 1976

REFERENCES

Pastor So and So
     Address and phone contact numbers here
Friend One
     Address and phone contact numbers here
Co-worker One
     Address and phone contact numbers here

STATEMENT OF FAITH – Peter and Paula Pastor

We Believe:

- The Scriptures of the Old and New Testaments are verbally inspired by God and inerrant and infallible in the original writings, and that they are of supreme and final authority. (2 Timothy 3:15-17; 2 Peter 1:21).

- There is only one God, eternally existent in three persons: Father, Son and Holy Spirit (Genesis 1:1; Deuteronomy 6:4; Matthew 28;19; John 10:30).

- In the deity of Christ (John 10:33); His virgin birth (Isaiah 7:14; Matthew 1:23; Luke 1:34-35); His sinless life (Hebrews 4:15; 7:26); His miracles (John 2:11); His vicarious and atoning death (1 Corinthians 15:3; Ephesians 1:7; Hebrews 2:9); His resurrection (John 11:25; 1 Corinthians 15:4); His ascension to the right hand of the Father (Mark 16:19); His personal return to earth in power and glory. (Acts 1:11; Revelation 19:11-16).

- In the absolute necessity of regeneration by the Holy Spirit for salvation because of the exceeding sinfulness of human nature, and that all are justified on the grounds of faith in the shed blood of Christ, and that only by God's grace, through faith alone, in Christ alone, are we saved (John 3:16-19, 5:24; Romans 3:23, 5:8-9; Ephesians 2:8-10; Titus 3:5).

- In the resurrection of both the saved and the lost; they that are saved unto the resurrection of life, and they that are not unto the resurrection of damnation. In the existence of a personal devil, who is still working in the world to destroy the souls of men, and that he and all of his angels will eternally perish in the lake of fire. (John 5:28-29; Matthew 25:41; John 10:10; 1 Peter 5:8).

- In the spiritual unity of believers in our Lord Jesus Christ (Romans 8:9; 1 Corinthians 12:12-13; Galatians 3:26-28).

- In the present ministry of the Holy Spirit by Whose indwelling the Christian is enabled to live a godly life (Romans 8:13-14; 1 Corinthians 3:16, 6:19-20; Ephesians 4:30, 5:18).

- In the Church, whose mission it is to proclaim the gospel to all the world, all of its endeavors being guided by multiple leadership and supported by the wise stewardship of God's people (Matthew 28:18-20; 1 Timothy 3:1-7, 5:17-18; Titus 1:5-9).

- That the ordinances of the Church, given by the Lord, are Baptism and Communion (Matthew 3:13-17, 28:19-20; Acts 10:47-48; Matthew 26:26-29; 1 Corinthians 11:23-26).

NOTES ON PETER PASTOR RÉSUMÉ

- Peter has his doctor's degree and has extensive experience as a pastor and ministerial director.
- Peter chose to include past secular experience on the résumé, but it could easily be left off with the extent of his ministerial experience and education.
- Peter included a statement of faith, as most pastors do.
- Although I don't generally recommend putting references on a résumé, Peter had plenty of space. It is not advisable to include more than three strong references. Everybody knows they're "canned" when they appear on your résumé.

In this space, please write down two or three points you like <u>best</u> about this résumé:

and two or three points you like <u>least</u> about this résumé:

Monte M. Missionary

1900 Anystreet Drive
Anytown, US 00000

Home Phone: 888-888-8888
Email: mmissionary@email.net

SUMMARY OF QUALIFICATIONS

- **Academically grounded** and **administratively gifted** missionary with **over 20 years** of well-rounded experience in ministry, technical applications, and management positions in a mission field context, including over 15 years of **cross-cultural** missionary experience
- **Strong spiritual conviction**, **commitment**, and **call** to serve the Lord; to build up His Kingdom and to equip believers for service
- **Passionate** about **training** and **coaching** national ministry/missions **leaders** in leadership, managerial, and technical aptitudes
- Exceptionally **skilled** in **developing partnerships** between organizations and government agencies to facilitate effective worldwide operations
- **Experienced** in **research** and **development** of **global ministry** programs
- **Earned MBA** in **Global Management** (Magna Cum Laude) March 2007

MINISTRY HISTORY & EXPERIENCE

Major Mission Organization, Central America   January 1994 to Present

Director of New Field Development [4/07 to Present]
- **Perform research** for new ministry field locations; **examining** the potential and opportunities within the new field regions for the initiation of MMO flight services
- **Conducted feasibility studies** in Guatemala and El Salvador, **consulting** national pastors, missionary organizations, national seminaries, and government agencies in efforts to **confirm** and **quantify ministry needs**

Director of Curriculum Development [1/05 to 3/07]
Seconded to MMO Asia
- **Conducted research** for the **formation** and **development** of CBT (computer based training) aviation curriculum for MMO worldwide operations
- **Consulted** directly with FAA, local training institutions, and aircraft companies for curriculum formation; **coordinated** training curriculum with MMO field managers

Chief Executive Officer (CEO), MMO Central America [3/03 to 12/04]
Seconded to MMO Central America, Bogata, Columbia
- **Conducted** CEO's responsibilities of **planning**, **organizing**, **controlling**, and **directing** the overall operation of MMO Central America
- **Coordinated** MMO Asia **leadership efforts** in formation of operational alliance between MMO Central America and MMO Asia
- **Maintained oversight** and **control** of **budgets** of all departments to ensure **accountability** and **accuracy** of assumptions, **quality** of projections and spending trends; **coordinated** and **maintained** oversight of MMO Central America national **fundraising** efforts, **assisting** in the **coordination** of **fundraising events** and the **production** of quarterly **newsletters**
- **Revised** MMO Central America **Board protocol** and **contract**, **establishing** primary quarterly and annual **goals** and **strategies**
- **Recruited** and **implemented** four **new** MMO Central America **Board members**

Director of Operations, MMO Central America [5/02 to 12/04]
- **Liaised** with church and mission community to **develop partnerships** with current and potential ministry users and with the Central American Civil Aviation authorities to **maintain** the current commercial **operating certificates** held by MMO Central America
- **Directed maintenance** and care of airplane fleet and **integrated** maintenance **procedures** which **reduced** aircraft **downtime; supervised construction** and **outfitting** of new MMO Central America hangar complex at International Airport
- **Produced** quarterly **reports** for MMO Central America board meetings and monthly progress reports for MMO Asia
- **Ensured** that company was in **compliance** with all Central America aviation and government **regulatory** and **licensing** agencies and took actions to **resolve deficiencies**; revised and formulated company policies to attain the **highest operating standards**

Program Manager Bolivia Program [4/99 to 12/00]
Bolivia Program
- **Liaised directly** with **departments** of the Bolivian Government, Bolivian Department of Civil Aviation, and the United Nations, to **maintain** Bolivian Program **operating status** in the country
- **Networked directly** with the local church and mission community to **develop** the existing **partnerships** and assist them in **reaching** their **ministry goals**
- **Responsible** for the **welfare** and **development** of the Bolivian Program **staff** consisting of four missionary families and 40 Bolivian workers

Director, Bolivian Aviation School [3/95 to 12/00]
- **Founded** and **directed** Bolivia Aviation School to comply with the Board mandate of nationalizing the Bolivia Program
- **Formulated** Aviation School **Policy Manual** and **compiled maintenance** and **flight curriculum** according to ICAO Standards
- **Recruited** Bolivian **students** and **instructed** for two years in elementary maintenance theory and practices

Chief Pilot [4/99 to 12/00]
Line Pilot / Mechanic [4/94 to 3/99]
- Fulfilled **flight duties** in **support** of three MMO bases and 40 airstrips throughout Bolivia; **supervised** crew scheduling
- **Supervised** the **construction** and **opening** of four **new airstrips** in Bolivia which allowed air access to missionaries living in remote areas
- **Performed** recurrent **pilot training** and **proficiency** flight **reviews** to maintain and upgrade staff pilot skills

Pre 1994 experience included:
- **Pilot/Mechanic** [1991-1993] with World Team in Ecuador in **support** of 10 remote **missionary** outpost **villages** along with the **maintenance** of two C185
- **Aircraft Maintenance Instructor** [1989] with Bible Institute Aviation in USA
- **Corporate Line Pilot** [1988] with major airline
- **Flight Instructor** [1987-1988] with a well-known flight school

EDUCATION & TRAINING

MBA Global Management, University of Anystate – March 2008. Graduated Magna Cum Laude (4.0 GPA)

B. S. Missionary Aviation Technology, Bible Institute Aviation, 1990. Received A & P Licenses

Diploma in International Ministries, Bible Institute, June 1986

Journeyman Machinist AA License, College of Applied Arts, 1982. Completed machinist apprenticeship (8000 hours)

FOREIGN LANGUAGES

Spanish: Speak/Read/Write

Indonesian: Conversational Speaking only

AVIATION LICENSES

- USA Commercial Pilot License
- USA A&P Mechanic's License

NOTES ON MONTE MISSIONARY RÉSUMÉ

- Monte is a very gifted administrative missionary and has extensive experience to document.
- Monte needed a strong summary of his qualifications that included a brief statement about his Christian walk and beliefs.
- Monte chose to go to three pages because of the extent of his education and experience. Had I been writing it for myself, I would likely attempt to find a way to refine it to two pages.
- Monte degree is mentioned in the qualifications summary, as well as in the Education and Training section.
- Because his responsibilities are quite broad, he needs a lot of detail so the reader can be fully aware of his gifts and talents.
- Monte needed key words highlighted in bold type so the reader has the opportunity to quickly scan for preliminary information, then come back and read the details.

In this space, please write down two or three points you like <u>best</u> about this résumé:

and two or three points you like <u>least</u> about this résumé:

MICHAEL MUSIC MINISTER

**0000 Hwy 395 ■ Anytown, US 00000 ■ 888-888-8888 Cell (Primary)
999-999-9999 Home ■ E-mail: michael.minister@church.org**

SUMMARY OF QUALIFICATIONS

- Have answered the Lord's call to serve in numerous areas of **music ministry** since 1992
- **Fifteen+ years** serving **as needed** as "fill-in" **music minister** in several area churches
- **Six+ years** serving **as needed** as a **"music evangelist"** during revival services at Anytown area churches; included working closely with various guest speakers and church members to **coordinate** all **music** for the services
- Accomplished **vocal soloist** and **capable guitarist**
- Successful **vocal coach/teacher**
- Additional skills include musical **transposition**, choral/instrumental **conducting**, worship service **preparation**, audio/visual **technician**, and group **leadership**
- Currently **working toward Master of Arts** in Religion (Biblical Studies Concentration)
- Earned **Bachelor's Degree in Music** (Vocal Performance Concentration)
- Studied **French** for **five years**, in addition to extensive **use** of many **other foreign languages** within pursuit of music degree

SUMMARY OF MINISTRY AND VOLUNTEER SERVICE

Christian Evangelical Church | *Anytown, Anystate* | 2001-present
- Served as **fill-in** as needed in the absence of the **Music Minister**
- Served as **music evangelist** for revival services

Anytown Baptist Church | *Anytown, Anystate* | 2001-present
- Served as **music evangelist** for revival services
- Served as guest **soloist**

Holy Baptist Church | *Anytown, Anystate* | 2001-present
- Served as **fill-in** while church was in search of **Music Minister**
- Served as guest **soloist**

Lovefilled Baptist Church | *Anytown, Anystate* | 2001–2004
- Served as **fill-in minister of music** on Sunday and Wednesday as needed
- **Director** of children's choir
- Member of adult **choir and praise team**
- Primary **ministry** was to assist in worship with **special music** during the service
- **Led** a personal **mission trip** to Indonesia to aid in the relief work after the tsunami

First Baptist Church | *Othertown, Anystate* | Summer 1995-December 2000
- Served as needed in the absence of the **Music Minister**

Othertown Baptist Church | *Othertown, Anystate* | 1992-present
- Served as needed in the absence of the **Music Minister**
- Served as guest **soloist**

Continued

SUMMARY OF EDUCATION AND SPECIALIZED TRAINING

Currently working toward Master of Arts in Religion (Biblical Studies Concentration)
Christian University (Christian Theological Seminary Distance Learning) | Fall 2007-present

Bachelor of Music | _University of Anystate_ | Fall 1995-Fall 2000
(Vocal Performance Concentration)
Course work included music theory, music history, composition, conducting, and
extensive vocal coaching
Member of university choir 1995-2000 under the direction of Dr. So and So. Toured
extensively throughout Europe and the U.S. Choir won numerous competitions,
including placing first in the annual _Gran Premio Europeo di Canto Chorale_ in
Gorizia, Italy, (the most prestigious choral competition in the world) in 1997
University of Anystate | Continued
Member of university opera theater group [1996-2000]
Chosen as featured tenor soloist for Bach Motet performance with the _Berlin Chamber
Orchestra_ [1996]
Solo vocal competitions included National Assoc. of Teachers of Singers, American Choral
Director's Association, National Federation of Music Clubs [1995-2000]

SUMMARY OF EMPLOYMENT

BIG ENERGY CORPORATION | _Anytown, Anystate_ | March 2001-present

Maintenance Operator, Local Chemical Plant
- Make routine checks on all equipment
- Run chemical tests
- Various other mechanical and plant operations duties

The Classy Apartments | _Anytown, Anystate_ | 1997-2001

Resident Manager, 50-unit apartment complex
- Responsible for troubleshooting all after-hour complaints and emergencies
- Performed monthly pest control procedures
- Serviced and changed filters on all AC units monthly

Anytown Construction | _Anytown, Anystate_ | 1996-2001

Construction Laborer
- Residential construction – new construction and remodeling projects
- Assisted with electrical, painting, plumbing, carpentry, sheetrock, brickwork, etc.

College Campus Church | _Anytown, Anystate_ | 1997-Dec 2000

Music Minister
- Directed adult and children's choirs
- Planned all music for worship services
- Planned and scheduled music for all holiday cantatas
- Lead (guitar accompaniment) praise and worship for youth Bible study

NOTES ON MICHAEL MINISTER RÉSUMÉ

- Michael has more volunteer service to the Lord than paid experience in the area of music ministry.
- He has earned his Bachelor's degree and is working on his Master's.
- Michael has had to work at secular employment to support his family and pay for his college, so his actual paid ministry experience is virtually non-existent.
- A glance through his strong qualifications summary, however, will interest the reader enough to finish reading the résumé and see that he is talented in the area of his calling.
- I set up his résumé so that the whole first page is related to music ministry.

In this space, please write down two or three points you like best about this résumé:

and two or three points you like least about this résumé:

Paul Youth Pastor
1010 Godspeed Blvd
Mytown, US 11111
555.555.1212
PaulYPastor@yahooland.com

SUMMARY OF QUALIFICATIONS

* Answering God's call to encourage and equip students to have a passion for the word of God by teaching them how to study God's Word, apply it to their lives, and intentionally share their faith with those around them
* Solid experience in leading, teaching, and facilitating student ministries
* Participated in summer missions, including discipleship studies, facilitating vacation Bible schools (assisting churches with planning, coordinating and completion), and evangelism
* Assisted in leading Young Disciple Bible studies two years in local community
* Strengths include professionalism, leadership ability, teaching ability, punctuality, and versatility
* Master of Arts in Christian Education

SUMMARY OF MINISTRY EXPERIENCE

Minister of Education | *Mytown Baptist Church* | Mytown, US | 2002-Present
* Lead, plan, implement and teach in all areas of student ministry, including: Sunday School, discipleship, Wednesday night worship, student FAITH ministry, activities, events, trips, and hospital visits for both students and adults
* Assist with Sunday School leadership meetings
* Provide oversight and facilitation of volunteers into our childcare ministry
* Lead the adult FAITH ministry
* Fill pulpit as needed when pastor is away

Bible Study Leader | *Christian Youth Camp* | Othertown, US | Summer 2001
* Led Bible studies for groups of 20-30 students in grades 11 and 12
* Facilitated outdoor recreation activities

Teacher/Athletic Director | *Christian High School* | Anytown, US | 2000-2001
* Taught Bible, math, language, and physical education, grades 9-12
* As athletic director, provided supervision of all athletic events, assisted with scheduling of games

Student Ministry | *Midtown Baptist Church* | Anytown, US | 1999-2000
* In charge of leading, planning, implementing, and teaching in all areas of the student ministry which included: Sunday School, discipleship, Wednesday night program, visitation, activities, events, and trips

EDUCATION

Master of Arts, Christian Education | Anystate Theological Seminary | 2001-2003
Bachelor of Arts, Religion | Great State University | Sometown, US | 1996-1999
Local Community College | Sometown, US   1995-1996
North Central Community College | Othertown, US 1994-1995

NOTES ON PAUL Y. PASTOR RÉSUMÉ

- Paul is a family man recently out of college.
- Paul's qualifications summary starts with a strong description of God's call on his life.
- Most of Paul's experience is in the area of youth ministry, so he needs to provide as many details as possible to set him apart from someone with the education, but less experience.
- Paul is qualified to apply for positions in either youth ministry or Christian education.
- Not all of Paul's experience is paid "work", but it is important that he list it because it is pertinent to the call he is answering.
- Much of Paul's experience has been gained as he worked his way through college, honoring what he believed was God's leading for him to get his degrees debt-free.

In this space, please write down two or three points you like <u>best</u> about this résumé:

and two or three points you like <u>least</u> about this résumé:

MARTIN MISSIONARY

0000 Holy Spirit Street
Anytown, US 11333
martin.missionary@missionary.org
555-555-1212

SUMMARY OF QUALIFICATIONS

- Eleven years serving the Lord in full-time international missions
- Extensive experience planning, coordinating, and facilitating short-term missions projects/teams
- Effectively trained Latin national employees in addition to as many as 250 team members annually from a broad variety of cultures and backgrounds
- Strong God-given leadership abilities; able to motivate a group of people and guide them to completion of the task at hand
- Positive attitude -- "I can do all things through Christ which strengthens me." Philippians 4:13
- Bachelor of Theology and Associate of Biblical Studies degrees
- Fluent in Spanish and gifted at relating to people from the Latin culture
- Comfortable in Microsoft Word, Excel and PowerPoint

SUMMARY OF MISSIONS-RELATED EXPERIENCE

Major Mission Org | Foreign Mission | July 2008 – Present

Volunteer Team Coordinator
- Prepared short-term team budgets and schedules
- Coordinated work/evangelism projects with U.S. churches and national pastors

Ministry Organization | Foreign Mission | August 2007 – June 2008

Global Teams Director (Partner Ministry of Major Mission Org)
- Managed short–term team department, coordinated short-term teams worldwide
- Planned and facilitated mission team projects in Bolivia

Major Mission Org | Foreign Mission | December 2002 – August 2007

Short–Term Team Coordinator [8/04 – 8/07]
- Facilitated short-term volunteer work teams (up to 250 volunteers per year dispatched in teams of up to 40 persons), working with national pastors
- Major ongoing projects included renovating a multi-story home into a 40-person guest house, remodeling four houses, and painting 10 missionary homes inside and out
- Teams also helped build a Christian school, built a Sunday-school building for a jungle village, painted a village school, and completed various additional community projects
- Provided follow-up evangelism ministry as needed

Major Mission Org, Continued

Hospital Maintenance Director [12/02 – 8/04]
- Managed national personnel and supervised daily maintenance for the hospital, school, and all missionary staff housing (10 missionary houses, local mission school, mission guest house, and all of the vehicles
- In charge of five full-time employees (24 hours) and three sub-contractors (negotiated contracts, set schedules, prepared maintenance budgets, and facilitated purchasing of supplies)
- Coordinated painting of jungle hospital over five-year period, including all rooms, surgery suites, offices, and waiting rooms

El Salvador Technical School | El Salvador, Central America | 1992 - 1998

Woodworking Teacher
- Taught construction carpentry, cabinetry, and furniture making at a Christian boys' vocational school

Previous experience includes 10 years in construction management

EDUCATION

- Bachelor of Theology | Anystate Theological Seminary
- Associate of Biblical Studies | Anystate Theological Seminary
- Spanish Language Institute | El Salvador 1996
- High School Graduate | Anytown, US 1975

PERSONAL INFORMATION

- Married (20 years)
- Three Children (2 boys, 1 girl)
- Denomination – GARBC Baptist
- Stateside Home Church – Calvary Baptist Church –Anytown, US

NOTES ON MARTIN MISSIONARY RÉSUMÉ

- Martin has solid missions experience in two foreign locations.
- Although he has secular experience in his past, he does not need to include it here in detail; so I simply made a one-line statement expressing the nature and length of his previous experience.
- Martin's "mission" included both building and maintaining facilities AND follow-up ministry after mission teams had been in and out of the facilities he managed, undertaking various projects and ministries.
- Personal information is not commonly put on a résumé today; however, in the case of missions and ministry, a pastor search committee or missions organization often wants to know whether the candidate has a family, if there are children at home, and how long the candidate has been married.

In this space, please write down two or three points you like <u>best</u> about this résumé:

and two or three points you like <u>least</u> about this résumé:

JANE SOCIAL WORKER

555 Anystreet
Anytown, AN 99!!!4
(123) 456-7890

SUMMARY OF QUALIFICATIONS

Christian psychiatric social worker offering three years of solid experience as a **behavioral science specialist** in the United States Military in addition to extensive education [including Bachelor's Degree] and comprehensive volunteer work in counseling and vocational guidance

PATIENT CARE AND ADMINISTRATION

Counseling, Testing and Evaluation
- Under close guidance, provided supportive counseling and/or follow up service to individuals experiencing a wide range of social or emotional problems [including adult adjustment, child and/or spousal abuse, drug and/or alcohol abuse, marriage difficulties, vocational counseling].
- Identified behavioral problems and psychological or substance use disorders.
- Conducted collateral interviews and screened records to obtain pertinent information.
- Recorded psychosocial data and behavioral observations in the form of social histories.
- Assessed client's present situation, mental status, and level of functioning.
- Assessed client's need for professional help.
- Maintained client's case records.
- Prepared and presented cases for agency staffing and supervisory conferences.
- Assisted in hospital discharge planning.
- Assisted with group counseling and therapy sessions and led discussion groups.
- Assisted in determination of need for hospitalization of emotionally disturbed or mentally ill clients.
- Administered, scored, and recorded selected achievement and objective personality tests and tests of organic impairment [under supervision of psychologist].

Consultation, Instruction and Administration
- Consulted with commanders and unit cadre on the management of individual behavioral problems.
- Provided commanders with general information on social/emotional problems and human services available in the military and civilian community.
- Provided instruction to agencies, units or groups on subjects related to health and welfare resources.
- Non-Commissioned Officer in Charge, Social Work Services, Army Hospital coordinating hospital staff and services with those of the Family Life Center [nine months].

Continued

RELATED PROFESSIONAL EXPERIENCE

- Currently performing **comprehensive volunteer counseling** at the Local Veterans Center in direct cooperation with any and all related agencies [including Job Service].

- Received hands-on experience [**two practicums** during most recent graduate studies] working with the State of Anystate Welfare Department including, but not limited to, **conducting interviews; providing** education/vocational **counseling, assistance** and **job placement** and **arranging transportation** for clients when necessary.

EMPLOYMENT HISTORY

United States Military
1979-1985

Behavioral Science Specialist 91G-20 • Multiple Assignments •

    Mental Hygiene Clinic • Anytown, Anystate [1982-1985]

    Family Life Center and Army Hospital • Any Military Base [1979-1982]

CONTINUING PROFESSIONAL STUDIES

- Will soon undertake correspondence study for MASTERS in Counseling [the only means by which this masters can be achieved in this State]
- Studied toward Masters in Social Work, University of Anystate, Anytown, Anystate • Fall 1982-Spring 1983

COMPLETED PROFESSIONAL STUDIES

Bachelor's Degree, Sociology and Psychology • East Central State University, Anytown, Anystate 1978

ADDITIONAL SKILLS

Fluent in Spanish

NOTES ON JANE SOCIAL WORKER RÉSUMÉ

- Bold job title immediately in Qualifications Summary. This person was only applying for positions as a psychiatric social worker. This wording choice immediately set her apart to the reader. If she applies to any company or organization that might find her status as a Christian offensive and, therefore, not call her for an interview, she should leave off the word Christian. Jane felt strongly about identifying herself as a Christian upfront.
- The bulk of the "bullet points" came directly from the job descriptions she was given where she worked. The terminology of the specific career field would be picked up in a software scan for keywords.
- Her "continuing professional studies" were separated from her "completed professional studies" so it was readily known that she was continuing to learn and grow in her profession.
- In today's market, I would likely change this font to Verdana for scanning/faxing clarity.
- Because she lived and worked in a geographical area where Spanish was commonly spoken, including the fact that she was fluent in Spanish was essential. If you are fluent in a foreign language, be sure to state it, even if you are not looking at foreign mission service.

In this space, please write down two or three points you like <u>best</u> about this résumé:

and two or three points you like <u>least</u> about this résumé:

Tammy T. Teacher

555 Anytown Lane | Anytown, US 00000
Home: 555-555-5555 | Cell: 555-666-6666
E-Mail: teacher@teachernet.com

SUMMARY OF QUALIFICATIONS

Teaching

- **B.A. in Biology**; **Minor: Physical Education**, Somestate College
- Somestate 4-12 Biology and K-12 Physical Education **residency certificate**
- **Seven years teaching** grades 9-12 science and physical education
- **Two years** as certified challenge course **facilitator** and substitute science instructor for Mountain Peak Learning Center (AASP)
- **One year 6th grade Science/Language Arts** teacher
- **Three years as K-12** substitute teacher
- Technology Committee **Chairperson**; Sophomore Class **Advisor**; Biology Club **Advisor**; **Master Teacher**, Grant **Writer**

Coaching

- **Seven years** as **head** varsity volleyball **coach** (9-12)
- **Two years** as **assistant** volleyball **coach** (9-12)
- **One year** as **assistant** middle school volleyball **coach** (8)
- **Three years** as volleyball recreational league **coach** (4-6)
- **Two years** as **head** middle school track **coach** (7-8)
- **Three years** as Science Olympiad **coach**

SUMMARY OF EXPERIENCE

Anytown Christian Academy   **1996-Present**

6th Grade Science and Language Arts Teacher | Fall 2007-Present | Anytown, US

- **Design** Christian-based lesson plans aligned with state GLEs for science and language arts
- **Implementation** of FOSS Science kits and STC Science kits
- **Member** of Science PLC Committee responsible for curriculum alignment
- **Handle** classroom management, parent communication, assessment, grading, and entering data into grade book software

Substitute Teacher | Fall 2003-Spring 2007 | Anytown, US

- Long-term substitute 4th grade [4/30/07 to 6/8/07]
- **Taught** prepared lesson plans to grades K-12 on call as needed
- Responsible for **classroom management**, **implementing** lesson plan prepared by classroom teacher, and additional duties as directed by the classroom teacher

Science and P.E. Teacher 9-12 | Fall 1996-Spring 2003 | Anytown, US

- Responsible for **designing** Christian-based **lesson plans** aligned with State learning requirements for science
- Handled **classroom management**, parent **communication**, **assessment**, grading, and entering data into gradebook software
- Served as **advisor** for various clubs
- Served as Science Olympiad (3 years) and volleyball **coach**
- Served as Technology Committee **chairperson**
- **Coordinated** Natural Resource Day with Dept. of Natural Resources four years
- **Co-grant writer** of two successful natural resource grants

Continued

Mountain Peak Learning Center   **Fall 2004-Summer 2007**

Challenge Course/Science Instructor | Anytown, US

- Mid-Level Leadership Camp **Instructor** [Summer 2007]
- Interim Asst. **Director** [Fall 2006] Coordinated and implemented schedules and events
- Home School Academy Science **Teacher** [Qtr 3, 06/07] Grades 7-12
- **Teach** creative hands-on Forestry and Water Ecology lessons to K-6 student groups in an environment that promotes student interest in the content area and emphasizes Biblical principals governing responsible stewardship
- As Challenge Course **Facilitator**, assist students in reaching their educational goals through problem solving and cooperation within the group

Othertown Christian High School   **Fall 1995**

Student Teacher | Othertown, US

- **Taught** Christian-based courses in Biology, P.E., and English
- **Designed** and **taught** creative lesson plans to grades 10-12
- **Served** as assistant volleyball coach

ADDITIONAL EXPERIENCE

Volunteer, Anytown Public Library Board Member Spring 2006-2007
Volunteer, Youth Group Instructor, Grades 6-8, St. Mary's Fall 2005-06
Assistant 8th Grade Volleyball Coach, Anytown Christian Academy 2005
Head Track Coach, Grades 7-8, Anytown Christian Academy 2004-2006
Head Varsity Volleyball Coach, Anytown Christian Academy 2000-Present
Assistant Volleyball Coach, Anytown Christian Academy 1996-1997
Field Experience, 2nd grade at-risk children, Othername Christian Elementary 1996
Head USA Volleyball Coach, grades 9-12, Club Othertown Volleyball 1996
Field Experience, 7th and 8th grade classroom, Christian Middle School 1994
Camp Counselor, National Youth's Sports Programs, Othertown 1993
Tutor, Somename Christian Youth Center, Othertown 1992-1993
Head USA Volleyball Coach, 7th and 8th grade Othertown Junior Academy 1991-1992

EDUCATION

Working on Pro Certification and Master's of Education | Anystate State University | Summer 2008
Bachelor of Arts, Biology | Sometown College | Othertown, US
Minor: Physical Education

HONORS AND AWARDS

- **6th Place State** Tournament finish Volleyball 2007
- **6th Place State** Tournament finish Volleyball 2006
- Freeman Invitational Tournament **winner** Volleyball Fall 2005
- **Sportsmanship Award**, Eaststate League Volleyball Fall 2005
- **Coach of the Year**, Eaststate League Volleyball Fall 2004
- Magic Apple **Grant Award** for Environmental Education April 2002
- **5th Place State** Tournament finish Volleyball November 2001
- Big **Grant Award** for $3,000 for Natural Resource Education Spring 2000
- **Teacher of the Month** May 1998 and May 1999
- **Who's Who Among America's Teachers** 1997 and 1998

Placement File available: January 1996
Educational Certification and Career Services Office
School of Education | Sometown College | Othertown, US 00000 | 555-777-7777

NOTES ON TAMMY TEACHER RÉSUMÉ

- This résumé is absolutely packed with information because she is both a Christian school teacher and a coach.
- Job titles appear first on the left to show consistency in career employment.
- Very concise entries describing duties allow for multiple positions held without taking up too much space. As a rule, someone reading the résumé of a school teacher will know approximately what that person does day to day. It doesn't all have to be explained in detail.
- She tells right up front what her certifications are so the prospective employer will know immediately if she is qualified.
- Because she is also a successful coach, the résumé is split out into two different areas. This creates a challenge, but it is important that all of this information is included because her acceptance of any position will likely hinge on there being a coaching position along with the teaching.
- Bold type highlights key words. If the résumé is to be scanned for keywords, however, one might wish to eliminate the bold type.

In this space, please write down two or three points you like <u>best</u> about this résumé:

and two or three points you like <u>least</u> about this résumé:

JOHN MORTGAGE LENDER

P. O. Box 123
Anytown, Otherstate 99!!!
(123) 456-7890 (M)

SUMMARY OF QUALIFICATIONS

Seventeen years in **banking**, project **management, consulting, training** and **appraisals** in addition to previous experience as a **university instructor**

PROFESSIONAL POSITIONS

Mortgage Lending • *Anystate Cooperative Credit Union* • Anytown, Anystate
• 5-88 to 8-89

Responsibilities included **all phases** of **mortgage lending** and **servicing**. Was additional involved in other phases of lending as required. Resigned to move to Otherstate.

Mortgage Lending • *Anytown State Bank* • Anytown, Anystate
• 10-85 to 1-88

Started the **mortgage department** at Anytown State Bank. Responsible for **all phases** of **mortgage lending**, including FHA, VA, conventional, commercial and construction loans. **Developed** all lending **policies** and **procedures** to comply with state and federal regulations. **Originated** and **sold mortgages** to the secondary market and performed other bank functions as required.

Real Estate • *Anytown Realty, Inc.* • Anytown, Anystate • 9-83 to 9-85

Full project **management** responsibilities, single family and commercial facilities. Full turn-key operation from securing property to completed facility acceptance. **Operated** own fee and appraisal and **consulting service** for investment properties. **Performed appraisals** for several local financial institutions and many corporations.

Mortgage Dept Consultant • *1st Bank of Anytown* • Anytown, Anystate
• 2-83 to 8-83

Hired as **consultant** to **evaluate, implement** and **improve efficiency** of mortgage department, including personnel, documentation, work blow and training.

Continued

Assistant Vice President • *Metropolitan Lending Bank* • Anytown, Anystate • 10-82 to 2-83

>This position was a result of a merger with Anystate Federal Savings & Loan Association and Metropolitan Lending. Responsibilities included **assisting** in the **management** of the Anytown **regional branch** office as well as **supervising** all phases of **mortgage lending** for the anytown **region** which included five other branches. **Developed** standardized **closing procedures** for the Metropolitan chain of **35 offices**.

Vice-President, Mortgage Lending • *Northern Federal Savings & Loan Assoc.* • Sometown, Otherstate • 1972-1982

>Responsibilities included **managing** all phases of **mortgage department** that included FHA, VA, conventional and commercial existing and new construction loans. **Developed** lending **policies** and **procedures** to comply with state and federal regulations. Also **developed** underwriting **standards** to conform with national markets. **Designed** appropriate mortgage **documents** to fulfill association's needs for flexible mortgage documents. **Developed** job **descriptions** with salary schedules for all departments of the association.

Instructor • *University of Anystate* • 1970-1972

>Instructor in Business Department. Assisted in expanding department to meet the needs of students and university. Subjects taught included Marketing, Management, Business Mathematics, Communications, Public Relations and Advertising.

U. S. Army • Secret Clearance • *Vietnam Veteran* • 1968-1970

PROFESSIONAL TRAINING

Seminar on Financing and Leasing Shopping Centers • Northwest Institute, Anytown, Anystate • 1984

Course I and II • Graduate Realtor Institute • 1984

School for Executive Development • University of Anystate • 1979, 1980

Leadership School • University of Anystate, Anytown, Anystate • 1978

Course 201-Society of RE Appraisers • Eastern America University • 1976

Course 101-Society of RE Appraisers • Eastern U.S. University • 1973

Numerous *workshops* and *management conferences* sponsored by the United States Savings & Loan League

Numerous *courses* through the United States Savings & Loan Institute

Continued

EDUCATION

Graduate Study • University of Anystate, Anytown, Anystate • Two Quarters • 1970

Bachelor of Arts • Business Ed. • University of Anystate, Anytown, Anystate • 1967

Associate of Arts • University of Anystate, Anytown, Anystate • 1965

Graduated • Anytown Senior High School , Anytown, Anystate • 1963

PERSONAL

Married • U.S. Citizen • Excellent Health • Past President of Anytown Board of Realtors • Past Director of Anystate Association of Realtors • Past President and Director of Anytown Kiwanis Club • Past Secretary of Anytown Country Club

NOTES ON JOHN MORTGAGE LENDER RÉSUMÉ

- Summary shows the wide scope of this gentleman's knowledge and expertise.
- Bold type highlights key words.
- Descriptive paragraphs include enough industry terms to make him stand out in a scan for keywords.
- Client chose to have the résumé at three pages despite my advice otherwise. Had I been able to make the choice, I would have done just enough to condense it to two pages without sacrificing any of the pertinent information.
- Client chose to include personal information on his résumé. Had I been able to make the choice, the personal information would have been omitted.
- John does not include his work phone on his résumé because his current employer does not know he is looking for another position at this time.

In this space, please write down two or three points you like <u>best</u> about this résumé:

and two or three points you like <u>least</u> about this résumé:

JANE BOOKKEEPER

P. O. Box 1234 • Anytown, AN 99!!!
(123) 456-7890

QUALIFICATIONS SUMMARY

➢ **A.A. Business Administration**
➢ Two years of comprehensive **full charge bookkeeping** experience with industrial service company
➢ Additional experience and training in **Office Management**

ACHIEVEMENTS SUMMARY

· Full Charge Bookkeeping ·

Included accounts receivable, accounts payable, billing, preparing and filing quarterly tax returns, writing monthly reports, maintaining company journal

· Office Management ·

Coordinated travel arrangements for employees, coordinated customer appointments with upper-level management schedule, periodically interviewed prospective employees, ordered supplies, acted as receptionist

· Computer Data Entry ·

In addition to using Apple computer system for effective completion of above-named responsibilities for Confidential Industrial Service Co., acted as assistant to professor in computer lab program during college, tutoring students in computer skills, primarily accounting related [some work with IBM system]

EXPERIENCE SUMMARY

Full Charge Bookkeeper • *Confidential Industrial Service Co.* • Anytown, Anystate • [1995-1997]

Computer Lab Assistant • *Anytown Community College* • [1993-1994]

EDUCATION SUMMARY

Associate of Applied Science, Business Administration • Anytown Community College, Received Degree 1994 • *Magna Cum Laude*

Small Business Management • Anytown Community College, Received Certificate 1994

Anytown High School • Anytown, Anystate • Graduated 1992 • With Honors

NOTES ON JANE BOOKKEEPER RÉSUMÉ

- Jane was going to apply for several types of jobs, so I broke out her EXPERIENCE into categories so the reader could see the various areas in which she had training and experience – predominantly full-charge bookkeeping and office management.
- Her Associate's degree in Business Administration was important enough to mention in the qualifications summary, especially since she did not have a lot of experience, being fairly freshly out of college.
- This is a semi "functional" résumé that focuses more on education and skills/areas of knowledge than the positions she has held (because of limited experience).

In this space, please write down two or three points you like <u>best</u> about this résumé:

and two or three points you like <u>least</u> about this résumé:

SUZIE GOSPEL SINGER

P. O. Box 111
Anytown, Anystate 00000
(111) 111-1111

PROFESSIONAL OBJECTIVE

Success as a **<u>Country</u> <u>Gospel</u> music entertainer** in today's highly-competitive gospel entertainment business. **Available for appearances on request**.

QUALIFICATIONS SUMMARY

Offering **twelve years** of **professional entertaining** experience including **opening shows** for **major performers**; **radio** and **fair** appearances; beauty **pageants**; **weddings**; company **parties**; charitable **benefits** and church **performances** •

PROFESSIONAL ACCOMPLISHMENTS

Major Performances

- Featured • **Nashville Video Showcase** • Nashville, Tennessee • 1992
- Featured • **Tennessee Hayride Jamboree** • Nashville, Tennessee •   1991
- Performed on the **Oklahoma Opry**, Oklahoma City, Oklahoma • 1991
- Appeared on the **Ralph Emery Show** in Nashville, Tennessee • 1991
- Performed **Opening Act** for **The Bellamy Brothers** in Anytown • 1991
- Performed **Opening Act** for **Sawyer Brown** On Tour • 1990
- Performed **Opening Act** for **The Kingston Trio** On Tour • 1989
- Performed **Opening Act** for **The Kendalls** On Tour • 1988
- Performed **Opening Act** for **Marie Osmond** On Tour • 1988

Significant Performances/Accomplishments

- Performed for **Air Base 50th Anniversary Celebration**; Anytown, Anystate • 1991
- Performed number with **Miss America** • Anytown, Anystate • 1991
- Appeared in Anytown **Chrysler/Dodge Television Commercial** • 1991
- **Director**, Twin Cities Production Showcases • 1989-Present
- Performed **Feature Act**, Anystate **State Fair** • 1991, 1990, 1988
- **Annual** Appearances For **Benefits** [Shriners Children, Booster Clubs, Talent Shows, etc.]

EDUCATIONAL TRAINING

- Completed **Take V Talent Studio** training for **Radio Voice Overs, Character Development, Product Handling**, Terminology, Duo **Commercials** and **Improvisation** • 1992
- Completed Live On Stage Workshop • 1990
- Completed Music Theory and Dance classes

NOTES ON SUZIE SINGER RÉSUMÉ

- Résumés for actors and singers are very much different than those for other types of employment.
- Suzie must highlight her successes, drop recognizable "famous" names if possible, list applicable training, and include all areas in which she is available for performances.
- The actor/singer résumé should ideally be one page and highlight only the most prestigious "gigs" or performances.

In this space, please write down two or three points you like <u>best</u> about this résumé:

and two or three points you like <u>least</u> about this résumé:

SALLY A. STUDENT

8888 Anyview Drive ~ Somecity, AN 66666
(555) 555-5555
e-mail: sallys@somemail.com

SUMMARY OF QUALIFICATIONS

o **Certified** alpine ski instructor with two seasons of experience as multi-age **instructor**, both **group** and **individual** instruction settings
o Interned as **office assistant** in busy high-school front office
o **Tutored** peers in Math and English
o Completed four **Running Start** classes at community college (during high school)
o Solid **microcomputer skills**, including Microsoft Word, PowerPoint, Excel and Publisher
o Maintain **3.85** GPA
o **Learn** new tasks **quickly**
o Able to **interact effectively** with persons of all ages from small children to senior citizens

SUMMARY OF EXPERIENCE

Office Assistant ~ Somecity H.S. ~ Somecity, Anystate ~ 2000-2001 school year

> Served as **office intern** in for-credit vocational training program (Community Resource Training) in busy high school front office ~ Duties included **typing** (Microsoft Word and Excel), **filing**, answering **telephone**, and **delivering messages** to students and staff ~

Dietary Aide ~ Somecity Care Center ~ Somecity, Anystate ~ 1999-2000 school year

> Nine month vocational work-study position **delivering** prepared **meals** from the hospital kitchen to the long-term care facility and **serving meals** to residents of the facility ~ **Assisted** in **clean-up** as necessary ~

Ski Instructor ~ Somecity Ski Village ~ Somecity, Anystate ~ Winters 1999 and 2000

> Provided both **group** and **individual instruction** to students in alpine downhill skiing ~ Taught **all ages**, <u>specializing</u> in children ages three to seven ~

Childcare Provider ~ Bob and Bonnie Someone ~ Somecity, Anystate ~ Summer 1999

> Provided **safe, supervised childcare** for three children, ages two to ten ~ **Prepared meals, scheduled** and **organized activities**, and **performed** light **housekeeping** as needed **nine hours per day** through the summer months ~

EDUCATION

Expected graduation June 2002 ~ Somecity High School ~ Somecity, Anystate

> **Course Highlights Include**:
>
> ❋ Accounting   ❋ Technical Mathematics
> ❋ Microcomputing   ❋ Diversified Occupations

NOTES ON SALLY STUDENT RÉSUMÉ

- High school students present a greater challenge as they often have little experience.
- Students should include transferable skills, hopefully excellent grades, leadership, volunteerism, community-minded attitude.
- Experience should include any volunteer positions, however insignificant they might seem, service as a team captain/manager, class or student body officer positions, internships, work-study positions, serving as a teacher's assistant, etc.
- If there is no experience, include ANY extra-curricular activities (including theatre productions, set design, costuming, makeup, providing sound systems for dances, concerts, etc; leadership clubs, outdoor clubs, FFA; athletics in any sport)
- Course highlights that are applicable to the type of work being applied for should be included if there is space.
- A high school student résumé should virtually never be more than one page. Don't fill up two pages with "blah blah blah" just to make it a two-page résumé. Only include pertinent information that will likely make a difference in whether or not a prospective employer will call you for an interview.
- A high school student's résumé could be done in the functional format if there is no work experience at all and only items such as extra-curricular activities, service as a team captain/manager, class or student body officer positions, internships, work-study positions, serving as a teacher's assistant, etc. are available to be included on the résumé.

In this space, please write down two or three points you like best about this résumé:

and two or three points you like least about this résumé:

VERBS AND MORE VERBS ~ Describing Skills. Watch overuse of a word. Be consistent. <u>Don't</u> say operat<u>ed</u>, revitaliz<u>ed</u>, utiliz<u>ing</u>, crea<u>ting</u>, negotiat<u>ed</u>. If it is a job you are no longer doing, keep it ALL <u>past tense</u> : operated, revitalized, utilized, created, negotiated. If it is a job you are currently doing, keep it ALL <u>present tense</u> : operating, revitalizing, utilizing, creating, negotiating.

achieved	constructed	estimated	launched	programmed	sewed
acted	contracted	evaluated	led	projected	shaped
adapted	contrasted	examined	learned	promoted	shared
addressed	controlled	expanded	lectured	proofread	showed
adjusted	converted	expedited	liaised	proposed	simplified
administered	corrected	explained	listed	protected	sized
advised	corresponded	expressed	located	provided	sketched
altered	counseled	extracted	maintained	publicized	sold
analyzed	created	fabricated	managed	published	solved
answered	critiqued	facilitated	marked	purchased	sorted
appraised	cultivated	filed	marketed	raised	specified
arbitrated	cut	financed	measured	received	spoke
arranged	decided	finalized	mediated	recommended	started
assembled	decreased	fixed	met	reconciled	streamlined
assessed	defined	followed	minimized	recorded	strengthened
audited	delegated	forecasted	modeled	recruited	studied
balanced	delivered	formulated	moderated	redesigned	summarized
broadened	demonstrated	founded	modernized	reduced	supervised
budgeted	described	gathered	modified	referred	supplied
built	designed	gave	monitored	refined	talked
calculated	detected	generated	motivated	rehabilitated	taught
calibrated	determined	guided	narrated	related	tended
catalogued	developed	hired	navigated	rendered	tested
categorized	devised	hosted	negotiated	reorganized	traced
chaired	diagnosed	identified	observed	repaired	trained
changed	differentiated	illustrated	obtained	reported	transcribed
charted	directed	implemented	opened	represented	transformed
checked	discovered	improved	operated	researched	translated
classified	dispensed	improvised	ordered	resolved	traveled
coordinated	displayed	incorporated	organized	responded	treated
coached	dissected	increased	oriented	restored	trimmed
collated	distributed	informed	originated	restructured	troubleshot
collected	diverted	initiated	oversaw	retrieved	tutored
combined	documented	inspected	painted	reviewed	typed
communicated	doubled	installed	performed	revised	uncovered
compared	drafted	instituted	persuaded	revitalized	unified
compiled	drew	instructed	photographed	sang	updated
completed	edited	integrated	piloted	saved	upgraded
composed	eliminated	interacted	planned	scheduled	used
computed	empathized	interpreted	predicted	searched	utilized
conceived	encouraged	interviewed	prepared	secured	verified
concluded	enforced	introduced	prescribed	selected	weighed
conducted	enhanced	invented	presented	separated	welded
configured	enlarged	investigated	printed	served	widened
considered	ensured	itemized	processed	serviced	won
consolidated	established	judged	produced	set	wrote

RÉSUMÉ INFORMATION WORKSHEET | The Information-Gathering Process – Step 2

Primary Trade or Chosen Field: _____

Number of Years of Experience: _____

Is this résumé for a job in your usual career area? Circle ONE: YES   NO

If NO, explain your career change plan: _____

_____

SECTION 1 - CONTACT INFORMATION

Full name as you wish it to appear on your résumé

_____

Residence Address (optional) _____

Permanent Mailing Address (or address at which you wish the prospective employer to contact you): _____

Home Phone #: _____ Work#: _____ (if you want to include it)

Do you wish your e-mail address to appear on your résumé? Yes _____ NO _____

If yes, your e-mail address: _____

SECTION 2 - SUMMARY OF QUALIFICATIONS

Note: You should write this LAST. You can better summarize when you've just reviewed all of your information. What will the prospective employer MOST need to know about you? List FOUR to EIGHT key, **skills,** *abilities*, **degrees**, or *certifications* in as few words as possible. (See the sample résumés in the previous study course section for ideas) Grab their attention! These may include the number of years of experience you have in your field, any supervisory positions, and your degree(s) if relevant.

- o
- o
- o
- o
- o
- o
- o
- o

SECTION 3 - SUMMARY OF EXPERIENCE

NOTE: Beginning with most RECENT:

EXAMPLE: Experience: **Anytown Clothing Store** mo/yr work began **8/82** mo/yr work terminated **8/92**, City **Anytown** State **Anystate** Supervisor **Hattie Blevins** Phone **555-8888** Position **Assistant Manager**

> Duties: **Hired, terminated** and **supervised up to 18** employees, prepared **employee** work **schedules, closed out** till and **prepared** bank **deposits, designed** and **implemented** window dressing **themes, supervised** inventory control, **processed** customer **orders** as needed.

PLEASE READ THIS BEFORE YOU GO ON! *See how much is said in how few words!* Note that there are no full sentences and that all of the tense is consistent throughout. Duties are outlined, specifics are quantified (supervising up to 18 employees), creativity is demonstrated.

Make a list of everything you did in any of your previous jobs in an ordinary day, an ordinary week, and/or an ordinary month. *Include* specific *duties that may be important to the position you are currently seeking.* What was most important? *Cross off things you believe they don't really need to know.*

THEN, prioritize duties listing the most important first *and the least important* last **in the order you would like the person reading your résumé to see them**. *They may only read the first three or four words* – ESPECIALLY MAKE YOUR FIRST WORDS IN EACH JOB-DESCRIPTION PARAGRAPH COUNT! *Priorities may change from résumé to résumé depending on the specific job opening for which you are using the résumé at the time – change them if necessary.* That's one of the great benefits of having computer word processing software.

Responsibilities in the above "Anytown Clothing Store" entry are prioritized beginning with those that are most important for the prospective employer to know. If you were applying for a sales clerk position rather than a management position for your next job, you might wish to reprioritize these items to highlight the customer service and cash register/bank deposit duties first and the other duties last.

Copy the jobs you want to use from your Skills and Abilities" worksheets. List MOST RECENT (or current) first and your OLDEST "job" last. **_Use more paper if needed._**

Experience 1:	Mo/yr work began:
City :	Mo/yr work terminated:
State :	Position:
Supervisor Name and Phone:	
Duties:	

Experience 2:	Mo/yr work began:
City :	Mo/yr work terminated:
State :	Position:
Supervisor Name and Phone:	
Duties:	

Experience 3:	Mo/yr work began:
City :	Mo/yr work terminated:
State :	Position:
Supervisor Name and Phone:	
Duties:	

Experience 4:	Mo/yr work began:
City :	Mo/yr work terminated:
State :	Position:
Supervisor Name and Phone:	
Duties:	

Experience 5:	Mo/yr work began:
City :	Mo/yr work terminated:
State :	Position:
Supervisor Name and Phone:	
Duties:	

Experience 6:	Mo/yr work began:
City :	Mo/yr work terminated:
State :	Position:
Supervisor Name and Phone:	
Duties:	

Experience 7:	Mo/yr work began:
City :	Mo/yr work terminated:
State :	Position:
Supervisor Name and Phone:	
Duties:	

Experience 8:	Mo/yr work began:
City :	Mo/yr work terminated:
State :	Position:
Supervisor Name and Phone:	
Duties:	

Experience 9:	Mo/yr work began:
City :	Mo/yr work terminated:
State :	Position:
Supervisor Name and Phone:	
Duties:	

SECTION 4 – EDUCATION - SPECIALIZED TRAINING - SPECIAL SKILLS

Degree(s), Name(s) of College(s), City, State, Year of college graduation

College #1 _____

_____

College #2 _____

_____

College #3 _____

_____

Name of School, City, State, Year of high school graduation *(for students, year of* <u>*expected*</u> *graduation)*

_____

On the résumé of a working adult, I generally include the name of school, city, state and year of high school graduation as a way of informally indicating approximately how old you are. Although age discrimination is not legal, it happens occasionally. It is your choice whether to include this information if you are a college graduate. Since I do not advocate including your age or other personal information on a résumé, this is one way of subtly conveying your age.

On the résumé of someone with a college degree, if space is a consideration, drop off the high school information. Persons with a college degree may choose to not include high school information for any reason. This is perfectly acceptable.

For high school students or recent graduates, list courses you've taken or activities you've participated in which are important to the job you are trying to get. *(See résumé samples for ideas)*

_____   _____

_____   _____

_____   _____

Special Skills (if any). These may include specifics on typing/computer/software ability, specifics on labor skills, foreign languages, artistic talent, etc. *Think in terms of what the prospective employer will want to know*. Are you an expert with Microsoft Excel? Are you good with photography? Do you speak Spanish? For students, did you help design the school annual or produce a PowerPoint presentation? Are you good with saws? Drills? Car maintenance? _____ _____ _____

_____ _____ _____ _____ _____

Hobbies/Interests: Optional and NOT RECOMMENDED.

You may include hobbies and interests if you feel strongly about it or if they are related to your line of work. **Most experts recommend they be left off**; and I do not take up space with them, personally, unless they mirror the client's occupation. It is your choice.

Résumé Writing Assignment

The purpose of this assignment is to write the résumé you will use in your search for God's next call for you or other job search. There are TWO parts to this assignment. <u>Please write the résumé based on your education, skills and experience as they are **today**.</u> THIS IS NOT A HYPOTHETICAL or FICTIONAL ACTIVITY.

❑ Part ONE: You <u>cannot</u> properly complete this assignment without completing your Skills Assessment Activities and Résumé WorkSheet FIRST!
   - By now you should have already carefully looked over the sample résumés. ***Your résumé should reflect your individual situation and should not look exactly any of these samples***.
   - <u>Do a quick review of the Résumé Crash Course</u> and then *write your résumé using* **what you have learned** *in the course and the information you have gathered in the skills assessments and on the worksheets.*
   - <u>After you have completed this assignment, I recommend that you wait at least 24 hours before you continue on to do the Final Revised Résumé assignment.</u> I virtually always "sit" on a résumé overnight and look at it again the next day with a "fresh eye" to make sure I haven't missed anything.
   - Have as many people as you like (friends, relatives, trusted co-workers) look over your résumé. Bear in mind, however, that not all of them will give you good advice on changes that should be made. Use your best judgment on what advice to accept and what to reject.

Once you have completed your résumé, you may wish to have Mrs. Jones (that's me) review and critique it for an additional fee of $12.95 US. If you wish to exercise this option, please e-mail me at ceo@wordcopro.com for additional details. ONLY clients who have purchased the 𝒴𝑜𝑢𝑟 𝑅é𝑠𝑢𝑚é: 𝒜 "𝒞𝑟𝑎𝑠𝑕 𝒞𝑜𝑢𝑟𝑠𝑒"© study course may exercise this option for $12.95. If you are not a "crash course client", my résumé critique or review fee is posted on my website at www.wordcopro.com.

❑ Part TWO: If you do not have letters of recommendation on hand (or if the ones you have are terribly outdated) initiate contact to obtain at least two *letters of recommendation* from previous employers who are willing and able to provide positive, constructive commentary on your skills and abilities.

If you have suitable letters of recommendation on hand, choose the two or three best ones for your current ministerial or missions call (or career aspirations) and photocopy them to send out with your résumé.

RESIGNATION LETTER/COVER LETTER

If you have previous experience writing resignation and/or cover letters, you may skip this assignment.

There are TWO parts to this assignment. *This is not a hypothetical activity*. <u>Check off each part as you do it</u>. The next page has a brief introduction to letters of resignation and cover letters. Read and study it before you begin.

❑ Part ONE: After reading the information provided, write a fictional *letter of resignation* addressed to your current church, missions organization, or employer. Inform him or her that you are resigning from your current position in six weeks. It is to be professional and typed. A sample letter of resignation is included in this assignment to use as a <u>guide</u>. Your letter should reflect YOU and your individual circumstances and should NOT look exactly like the sample.

❑ Part TWO: After reading the information provided, type a *cover letter* to accompany your résumé. Your cover letter may be addressed to either a real or a fictional church, missions organization, or company, but should be written as though you were applying for a job TODAY with your current skills and knowledge. Two sample cover letters are included in this assignment <u>to use as a guide – one for a soon-to-be high school graduate and one for an older, working adult</u>. Your letter should NOT look exactly like either sample and should reflect YOU and your skills and abilities as relate to any job you may choose. You may wish to review your Skills Statement for ideas of information you may want to include.

Writing a Resignation Letter

A resignation letter is a formal courtesy extended to your present church, missions organization, or other employer when you are preparing to leave your position. When you send it will depend on the terms of your current employment contract or agreement. Some terms of employment have different periods of time that must be given in the way of severance notice (commonly two to six weeks).

Please make sure you take this step in a timely manner. It is extremely important to make this letter positive and respectful. Whether or not you're leaving on good terms, the church, organization, company or someone who works there may be beneficial to you later on as a reference, as a networking partner, or even as a client if you were to become an independent contractor or consultant. Don't "burn any bridges" with this letter — you may be sorry later. You're a Christian, think "WWJD?"

It is a good idea to thank the church, organization, or company, and your supervisor specifically (if applicable), for the knowledge and skills you gained while employed there. Regardless of whether your experience was entirely good or bad, there are always things you learned at any position that will benefit you throughout the rest of your Christian service or working life.

> Don't "burn any bridges" with this letter. You're a Christian, think "WWJD?"

The resignation letter you write for this assignment should be addressed to your current church, missions organization, or employer, informing him or her that you are resigning your position in six weeks (even if you're not) and expressing your thanks for the skills you have been taught and the valuable experience you gained. If you are not currently employed, make something up.

If you are doing this assignment (or the whole course) on a computer at church and your pastor doesn't know you're thinking about answering God's call to serve elsewhere, make sure that you don't "surprise" your pastor and church family by leaving a copy of a "sample" letter in the trash or on the computer hard drive. You should be totally upfront with your current church, organization or employer unless there's absolutely no way around it. If, for whatever reason, you believe you cannot confide in them, you will have to pray about it and seek God's peace in your decision.

Writing a Cover Letter

A cover letter is a tool you use to both accompany and complement your résumé. It usually either gives additional details that may not appear in your résumé or it highlights details that do appear in your résumé that you want to make sure the reader doesn't miss (or both). It is most commonly used for two things:

- Point by point tie your experience and knowledge into the specific requirements advertised for a position or posting

- Explain gaps in your employment history, changes in your career itself, or moves to a new state or town

This letter should be "short and sweet" — usually three or four paragraphs. The amount of detail your cover letter contains will depend on the position you are applying for, the skills and knowledge you have to offer, and the circumstances and events of your past and present Christian service or working life. Each cover letter should be written specifically for a position. Although it is more commonly done than you might think, you should never use a "generic" cover letter. If you are in ministry or missions, one of these paragraphs must briefly make it clear you are theologically "on the same page.

Your cover letter should either identify the position you are applying for (*see example*) or state a general objective if there is NOT a specific opening at this time (*Enclosed is my résumé to be placed on file for a possible future opening as a _____ with your church, organization, or firm.*) Keep in mind that in today's competitive job market, having something in an organization or employer's hands on any given day may get you a shot at a position they didn't even know was going to be open yesterday.

You should refer the "reader" to your résumé as well as state specific points that tie your experience and education into the requirements for the position (if known). It pays to do some research to find out the specifics of a particular position with this church, organization, or company.

> **First paragraph:** Inform the church, organization, or company you are sending your résumé and/or application and why.

... absolutely do NOT make it sound like you copied it out of a book.

> **Second (and sometimes third) paragraph**: State how your skills and knowledge fit into the position requirements, (or if you don't have exact skills and knowledge, explain how the skills and knowledge you DO have can be adapted to their requirements), and express to them why you believe you are the right person for the position and why you are a BETTER choice than anyone else they may be considering. Explain if and why you are relocating or if there are special or extraordinary circumstances that resulted in your leaving your last (or any) position.

> **Final paragraph:** Let them know that they are welcome to contact you for further information if needed or to set up an interview appointment on a time and day that is convenient for both of you. Thank them for considering you for the position.

Avoid lots of big words and going on and on with thank-yous. Make it businesslike and friendly. **<u>But absolutely do NOT make it sound like you copied it out of a book</u>**. Examples provided here are for general guidelines. Your finished cover letter(s) should not look exactly like any of the samples in this assignment.

If at all possible, it is best to have your cover letter on the same paper and in the same font with the same "letterhead" as your résumé.

> The amount of detail your cover letter contains will depend on the position you are applying for, the skills and knowledge you have to offer, and the circumstances and events of your past and present Christian service or working life.

The resignation letter and cover letters that follow are examples to give you insight into possibilities for wording and layout. Please do NOT use these exact letters for your own resignation or cover letters. Your resignation letter will reflect the specific circumstances by which you are leaving your current church, organization or other employer. You will need to carefully review the points you noted in your skills summary and use that as the base for your cover letter.

The rest of this page is intentionally left blank in case you want to sketch out the main points you don't want to forget to cover in your letters.

Paul Youth Pastor
1010 Godspeed Blvd
Mytown, US 11111
555.555.1212
PaulYPastor@yahooland.com

Whenever 9, 2009

Bob Smith
Senior Pastor
Calvary Christian Fellowship
01010 Somethingview Lane
Somecity, AN 00000

Re: Resignation

Dear Pastor Smith:

This letter is to inform you that I am resigning my position as assistant youth pastor as of June 5. Experiences like this are important to my future service to our Lord, and I truly appreciate the opportunities I have had at CCF to stretch and grow in my faith. It is my firm belief that God is calling me to ministry in an inner-city setting, so I will be seeking His direction toward answering that call.

The time and effort you have put in as a trainer, mentor and spiritual leader so that I could more fully serve the Lord for the advancement of His kingdom are much appreciated. Your Christian walk has been an inspiration to me, and I will be a better youth pastor because of my time spent with you and the rest of the CCF staff.

I would like to request that you write a letter of recommendation for me to keep on file for future employment opportunities. You may send it to the address on this letterhead or get it to me by inter-office mail before my last day of work.

In Christ,

Paul Y. Pastor

Paul Youth Pastor
1010 Godspeed Blvd
Mytown, US 11111
555.555.1212
PaulYPastor@yahooland.com

Whenever 9, 2009

Bob Smith
Pastor Search Committee Chairman
Calvary Christian Fellowship
01010 Somethingview Lane
Somecity, AN 00000

Re: Position opening, Assistant Youth Pastor

Dear Mr. Smith:

In response to your posting on *Christianemployment.com*, my résumé is enclosed for your review for the position of Senior Youth Pastor with your church. CCF is well-known to be a spirit-filled body of believers, with a solid focus on outreach, both in the community and globally. Upon reviewing your statement of faith and your qualifications for the position, I believe I should be a "good fit" for this opening.

You will note on my résumé that I have over 10 years of experience, as well as a Master's in Christian Education. My short-term missions experience includes three trips to Mexico to work on a team building houses and doing community outreach follow-up. Because I have worked my way through college (to honor God's desire for my family to be debt-free), much of my "work" experience is not "ministry-related". However, I have a clear call from the Lord on my life to be in youth ministry at this time.

My wife, Susie, and I have two young children and are praying for just the right place for God to put us to serve Him and "settle in". My wife plays the keyboard and I play guitar; and we both sing. We have a number of youth programs that have been successful in the past that we'd like to share with you at an interview.

Contact information is provided above should you need further information or desire to arrange a mutually satisfactory interview appointment date and time. We trust the Lord in His plan for our lives, and look forward to hearing from you.

Sincerely,

Paul Y. Pastor

Enclosure

JOHN MORTGAGE LENDER
P. O. Box 123
Anytown, Otherstate 99!!!
(123) 456-7890 (M)
e-mail: jml@youknowwhat.net

Whenever 9, 2008

Bob Smith, President
S & S Credit Union
01010 Somethingview Lane
Somecity, AN 00000

Re: Position opening, Loan Officer

Dear Mr. Smith:

In response to your advertisement in *The Somecity Gazette*, my résumé is enclosed for your review for the position of Loan Officer with your firm. S & S has a solid reputation for quality customer service and fairness in its dealings, and is highly respected throughout the industry. After closely examining your posting, I have determined that my qualifications appear to be right in line with the specifications you have laid out for this position.

You will note on my résumé that I have seventeen years of experience in banking, project management, consulting, training and appraisals in addition to experience as a university instructor. My familiarity with all phases of mortgage lending, coupled with knowledge in the areas of project management and appraisals, makes me an ideal candidate for this position.

Due to health concerns for our aging parents, I am relocating my family to Anystate to be available to assist in their care. Family is important to me, and I know that S & S is a solid, family-oriented banking institution.

Contact information is provided above should you need further information or desire to arrange a mutually satisfactory interview appointment date and time. Thank you for your consideration of my qualifications for this position, and I look forward to hearing from you.

Sincerely,

John M. Lender

Enclosure

SALLY A. STUDENT
8888 Anyview Drive
Somecity, AN 66666
(555) 555-5555
e-mail: sallys@somemail.com

Whenever 9, 2008

Bob Smith, Vice President
S & S, Inc.
01010 Somethingview Lane
Somecity, AN 00000

Re: Position opening, Physicist Internship

Dear Mr. Smith:

In response to your advertisement in *The Somecity Review*, my résumé is enclosed for your review for the position of Level I Physicist with your firm. Your company's training program for physicists and engineers is highly respected throughout the industry, and I am confident that this placement is just what I need to round out my experience and education.

Following high school graduation (June 2008), I will be enrolling at Anystate University. Please note that I plan to major in physics and have participated in several research projects in school. My related education, coupled with an eye for detail, the ability to work well with people of all ages, and the capability to learn new tasks quickly, should make me a good candidate for this position/program.

Contact information is provided above should you need further information or desire to arrange a mutually satisfactory interview appointment date and time. Thank you for your consideration for this position and I look forward to hearing from you.

Sincerely,

Sally A. Student

Enclosure

RÉSUMÉ REVIEW – THE FINAL STEP

❑ Look over the Revision Worksheet on the next page to review what points are most important to be covered on your résumé in terms of layout and content.

❑ If you have identified problem areas, list them and write out your proposed solutions to the problems.

❑ Based on the problems you identified in your study of the Revision Worksheet and the solutions you have proposed, make what you believe are necessary corrections to your résumé.

❑ Check off each item on the Revision Worksheet to verify your résumé is now the best it can be.

❑ PLEASE, don't forget to do an additional proofread of your résumé after you have made any changes.

RÉSUMÉ REVISION WORKSHEET

❖ You now need to carefully review your résumé. Revising your résumé is a technical/informational writing task.

❖ Check off each item as you do a step-by-step review of your completed résumé.

❖ You may wish to photocopy this sheet before you begin and have one or more persons use it as a tool with which to assist you in evaluating your résumé.

Formatting (Layout)

☐ The layout is attractive and doesn't appear "cluttered"; the information is easy to read and understand

☐ The font is simple and readable – especially if I am sending it to companies/organizations that may run it through scanning software

☐ Headings/subheadings/important points are in boldface or larger type (UNLESS I am sending it to companies/organizations that may run it through scanning software)

☐ Adequate spacing is provided between lines; the text is carefully edited and is error free; the résumé is as short as possible without appearing cramped

Organization of Your Résumé

☐ Information is organized so it can be read easily and quickly

☐ The most important and most recent information is presented near the top and near the beginning of paragraphs

☐ The various elements of the résumé are presented in a way that highlights my strengths

Content of Your Résumé

☐ Information is accurate and verifiable – no misrepresentations

☐ Information is presented clearly – no potential for confusion

☐ My strengths are highlighted and are <u>easy to spot</u>

☐ Specific details, such as dates and facts, are provided as needed

Terminology and Writing Style

☐ Statements are brief and begin with action words that demonstrate my accomplishments and describe my results

☐ An upbeat "voice" conveys excitement for work, confidence in my abilities; and, if appropriate, my love for the Lord

☐ Language is clear and concise – tense is consistent throughout (past tense for previous positions, present tense for current position) – industry terminology is included, if applicable

List any problem areas you identified:

How do you plan to resolve these problems?

YOU'RE ALMOST DONE!!

PRINT OUT YOUR REVISED RÉSUMÉ AND ASK SEVERAL FRIENDS, FAMILY MEMBERS AND/OR CO-WORKERS TO READ THROUGH IT FOR TYPOGRAPHICAL ERRORS AND/OR INCONSISTENCIES. Invite them to use copies of the Revision Sheet if you like.

My general rule for examining a résumé is to look at it one day, then "sleep on it" and look at it again the next day with a "fresh eye". This almost always works to catch errors such as mistyped dates, a key area of knowledge or skill that you've omitted, or a formatting inconsistency.

My recommendation is that you do not write your final cover letter(s) until after you have done the résumé review. You will be less likely to leave any important points out of your cover letter.

Remember that you may need to reprioritize your qualifications summary for each application you submit, depending on your qualifications and the type of job you're applying for. Once again, consider what the prospective church, organization or employer most needs to know about your beliefs, your education, your skills & abilities, and your areas of special knowledge.

You may also need to reprioritize the duties listed in each job description paragraph so that the reader sees FIRST what you most want him or her to know about you. Don't take any chances on the reader missing important information by it not being in the right place for a several-second eye scan.

And remember, you can't be too "nitpicky" about how it looks — consistency in spacing, consistency in grammar, consistency in formatting. This is a COMPETITION (even in Christian ministry), don't forget!

A QUICK WORD ABOUT PAPER

There are so many papers available today, it positively boggles the mind. Choose a quality paper that is tasteful for your line of work. Unless you are a web designer or an actor, you will likely want to stay with a conservative paper that shows you off as the professional you are.

I recommend that you transport and/or mail your résumé in a large manila envelope to keep it straight and unfolded. Let your résumé be the only one in the pile that is beautifully straight and doesn't have fold lines in it. (This is also important if your résumé will be run through a scanner by the employer. Papers that have been folded NEVER scan as well as those that are completely flat) With all of the other factors excluded, it may be the one thing that stands out and gets your résumé to the top of the pile to be reviewed by a prospective employer.

Try to use the same paper for all related documents, including supplemental information sheets (References, Salary History, College Courses Completed, Certifications, etc.) and cover letters.

CURRICULUM VITÆ

Curriculum vitæ is a document that resembles a résumé, but contains MUCH more detail and information. It is most commonly used by individuals who have been published extensively and have a PhD. Curriculum vitæ may be up to 14 pages long, depending on the circumstances. If you have been asked to provide curriculum vitæ to a prospective employer, do some research online to see what it really entails. If you have a PhD, you probably already know what it is and whether you need one.

.PDF

In today's world, even among churches and missions organizations, the .pdf file is a valuable tool for the job-seeker. Because there are so many differences in versions of leading software (MS Word and WordPerfect), along with Open Office thrown into the picture, it can be a very good idea to convert your résumé and accompanying documents to Adobe® Acrobat® .pdf format so they can be opened and read in their exact form by anyone who has a recent version of Adobe® Acrobat® Reader.

Résumé Survey Chart

For each résumé you send out, please fill in the following information. **Sent to** = company name; **Info From** = newspaper ad? Job Service or WorkSource listing? In-house posting? Etc.; **Response** = did you receive a response? Positive or negative? Date of interview appointment or follow-up? _We recommend you keep this original in your study course and photocopy it as you need it._ Hopefully, you will have your dream job before you finish the first page!

Date	Sent To	Position	Response?	Interview?

Page _____ of _____

You made it !!

Thank you for purchasing my résumé writing study course. Should you have questions or desire to have me proofread or critique your completed résumé for you, visit my website at www.wordcopro.com or e-mail me at ceo@wordcopro.com.

I will be happy to assist you in any way possible. My fees for proofreading and critiquing are listed on my web page or are available by request via e-mail. For your own benefit and record-keeping, please fill out the self-evaluation certificate below.

Gretchen Slinker Jones
Wordcopro.com

SELF-EVALUATION AND CERTIFICATE OF COMPLETION

Completed each section of the study course in order: Circle one   YES   NO

If you skipped a section, please briefly explain why:

What could I have done better in completing the study course?

Did this have an effect on how my résumé turned out? If so, why?

Date I completed the study course _____ .

Don't forget that additional lessons on Goal Setting, Interviewing, and Online Job Searching are available from wordcopro.com online.

About the Author

Gretchen Slinker Jones was raised and educated in Southwest Idaho and will never quit studying English and Writing. She spent 17 years in Southcentral Alaska before moving to the "Inland Northwest" in the late 1990s, settling on the fringe of the beautiful Selkirk mountain range. The owner of a desktop publishing and business writing firm, she specializes in résumé writing for clients all over the globe. She has been teaching résumé writing for over 20 years. Jones' freelance writing projects have included a weekly newspaper column for five years and a number of newspaper articles.

Jones is working on a historical novel set in her native Idaho and writes poetry for adults and children, as well as children's short stories. Her poems (including several that won awards and honors) have appeared in numerous anthologies, newspapers and magazines; and virtually all of them are currently available in *Song of the Heart: The Complete Collection* ISBN: 978-1441496621. She wrote *Breastfeeding: A Mother's Guide* in 1984 and revised it in 1989. It was "re-released" in the spring of 2009; ISBN: 978-1441499103. Current writing projects at the time this book is published are a 2nd volume of *Selkirk Mountain Inspiration* and two non-fiction books.

You may find Jones on the web at www.wordcopro.com and www.selkirkmountainmemories.com.

CPSIA information can be obtained at www.ICGtesting.com
Printed in the USA
LVOW120221261111

256344LV00004B/28/P